SPORTS HEROES WHO WOULDN'T QUIT

The dramatic stories of fifteen courageous athletes who overcame seemingly hopeless odds and displayed tremendous
courage and fortitude to "make it" in the sports of their
choice. Major league baseball players Gene Bearden, Mickey
Mantle, Red Schoendienst, Jackie Robinson and one-armed
Pete Gray . . . channel swimmer Gertrude Ederle . . .
golfers Ben Hogan and Ken Venturi . . . hockey player
Gordie Howe . . . boxer Henry Armstrong . . . football
players Doak Walker and quarterback Johnny Unitas . . .
the "little" jockey Conn McCreary . . . runner Glenn Cunningham . . . basketball player Bob Cousy. Their success in
today's competitive world of sports makes exciting reading
for sports fans.

BOOKS BY HAL BUTLER

Sports Heroes Who Wouldn't Quit

by hal butler

JULIAN MESSNER
NEW YORK

Published by Julian Messner
a division of Simon & Schuster, Inc.
1 West 39th Street, New York, N.Y. 10018
All Rights Reserved

Third Printing, 1974

Photos of Pete Gray, Henry Armstrong,
Gertrude Ederle and Conn McCreary
courtesy United Press International
Photo of Glenn Cunningham courtesy Duke D'Ambra

Library of Congress Cataloging in Publication Data

Butler, Hal.
    Sports heroes who wouldn't quit.

    SUMMARY: traces the careers of fourteen men and one woman
who succeeded or made spectacular comebacks in professional
sports despite physical handicaps, illness, or injury.
    1. Athletes, American—Biography—Juvenile literature.
2. Sports—United States—Biography—Juvenile literature.
[1. Athletes] I. Title.
GV697.A1B82 1973   796′.092′2 [920]   72-11821
ISBN 0-671-32581-7
ISBN 0-671-32582-5 (lib. bdg.)

Printed in the United States of America   102486

CONTENTS

Introduction

The rigid, uncompromising demands that sport places on its participants is probably greater today than it has ever been. To make it in the "big time"—whether in baseball, football, basketball, hockey or one of the so-called minor sports—requires not only dedication to the game but superb physical fitness, mental alertness and stamina.

It seems incredible that any man with less than normal faculties could ever make good in today's competitive sports. But some—with more grit and determination than others—have done so.

Some athletes have suffered childhood injuries that, by all odds, should have eliminated them from participation in sports—but they have overcome their misfortunes to reach stardom. Others have been cut down in mid-career by serious injury or illness—and have fought their way back. And many have been considered "too small" to participate with the big men of modern sport—and have battled their way to the top.

This is the story of fifteen courageous athletes who overcame seemingly hopeless odds to make it big in the sport of their choice.

I tip my hat to them.

Hal Butler

1
Gene Bearden . . .
war casualty on the mound

The year was 1943. The place was the vast expanse of the South Pacific. World War II was raging, and the United States Navy had penetrated the southern reaches of the Pacific Ocean despite the battering it had taken at Pearl Harbor on December 7, 1941. But the going was rough. The Japanese Navy was powerful and alert, and its submarines were a deadly menace.

The United States cruiser *Helena* rolled in a choppy sea "somewhere in the Pacific"—a secretive wartime description always given to American ships prowling those southern waters. She was about to be torpedoed, but her crewmen did not know it. The commander of a Japanese submarine already had the *Helena* firmly zeroed in on his periscope. He watched the cruiser for a moment with deep satisfaction and then gave the command to fire. The sleek, blunt-nosed torpedo slashed a path through the green water and headed for the *Helena* amidships.

Working in the engine room of the *Helena*, along with others, was Henry Eugene Bearden, a 23-year-old sailor who had been uprooted from his home in Lexa, Arkansas, to serve his country in the war against Germany and Japan. He was unaware, of course, that a great calamity was about to ensue. He did not know that in the next few seconds he would be almost killed, ripped apart in the manner of a rag doll torn by a child.

The torpedo struck. The explosion tore a gaping hole in the *Helena,* and young Bearden was blown out of the engine room into the sea, his fine young body savagely mangled. He spent ten pain-ridden, semi-conscious days clinging to wreckage in the sea before he was picked up and rushed to a hospital. Navy surgeons did what they could for him. They patched him up like an old piece of clothing, putting an aluminum plate in his head and in his left leg to substitute for skin and bones that were no longer there. He was presented with the Purple Heart, but he was not presented with much hope. Doctors said that he had little chance of living, but if he did, he "would not be worth much." It was either death or the frustrating life of a cripple.

Henry Eugene Bearden lived, and in time he was sent back to the States, his war days over. He walked with a limp now, but it did not keep him from thinking about a career in baseball. He decided to keep the extent of his injuries as much a secret as possible, because he feared that he would not be given a fair chance if baseball men knew he was so badly injured. Through sheer dedication and determination, Bearden caught on with two farm clubs belonging to the Cleveland Indians. In 1947 the young left-hander pitched for Oakland, then in the Pacific Coast League and managed by Casey Stengel. Mostly on the strength of a baffling knuckleball, he won sixteen games and lost seven that year—and although he was unable to hide the aluminum patchwork in his head and on his leg from his teammates, he never really revealed how badly he had been hurt or how close to death he had come.

Late in the 1947 season the Cleveland Indians called Bearden (he was called Gene Bearden now) up to the home club for a tryout. Lou Boudreau, the shortstop-manager of the Indians, wasn't impressed. Bearden pitched one-third of an inning, walked one batter, allowed two hits, was charged with three runs and promptly was sent to the showers.

It had been an incredibly poor performance, but despite this fact his 16-7 minor-league pitching record earned him a chance to report to the Cleveland Indians for spring training in 1948.

One day the Indians were playing a preseason game with the New York Giants at Phoenix, Arizona. Bearden was pitching, and he was not doing well. At one point the Giants loaded the bases with one out, and a disgusted Boudreau trudged from his shortstop position to the mound. He had just about had enough of Mr. Bearden.

"Well," he said in an ugly voice, "do you want to get out of here right now or do you want to keep on pitching?"

Bearden looked the distraught manager squarely in the eye. The towering ambition that had been driving him came to his mind before he answered. *I want to pitch major league ball,* he said to himself. *I have to prove to myself as well as others that I can do it.*

Bearden replied in a steady voice.

"If I get out of here right now, I know I'll never get back in again," he said. "So I'll keep on pitching."

"All right then—pitch!" snapped Boudreau.

Bearden pitched. He struck out the next two batters, retiring the side with three runners stranded on the bags.

That display of sheer guts made up Boudreau's mind for

him. He would take Gene Bearden north with the club. Maybe, after all, he could help the team.

Help was hardly the right word. He *led* the team. Inspired by Boudreau's confidence in him, Bearden won twenty games for the Indians, losing only seven, and was a major factor in keeping Cleveland in the pennant race. And when the chips were down—at the end of the season and in the World Series —the young man who had been pronounced either a dead man or a hopeless cripple was at his best.

As the American League race ground down to its last few days, the Cleveland Indians and the Boston Red Sox were in a virtual tie for first place. Cleveland had a critical three-game series with the Detroit Tigers to close out the season, and Boudreau threw his two top pitchers at the Tigers in the first two games—Bob Feller and Bob Lemon. The Tigers beat them both.

That put Cleveland on the spot. They had to win the last game against the Tigers. If they did, they would tie the Red Sox for first place and bring about the first American League playoff game in history. If they lost, they were out of it.

Boudreau sent Gene Bearden to the mound. And Bearden did what Feller and Lemon were unable to do—he pitched a superb game and shut out the Tigers 8-0.

The victory brought about a one-game play-off between the Indians and Red Sox to decide the pennant.

There was one idle day before the play-off game at Fenway Park in Boston. Boudreau worried over which pitcher to start in this final, all-decisive game. By game-time, Feller would have three days' rest behind him, Lemon two and Bearden only one. It was logical to think that Feller should be the man. But Feller had failed to halt the Tigers, and so had Lemon.

Bearden's knuckleball, though, had baffled them. Boudreau approached Gene Bearden.

"Do you think you could go with one day's rest?" he asked.

"I think I can, Skip," Bearden said.

Boudreau nodded. "It's your ballgame," he said.

It was a tough situation for any pitcher. But it was another opportunity for Bearden to prove that metal plates in his body did not necessarily rule him out as a ballplayer. That was the way he had to look at it.

For the first few innings the game was close. Cleveland scored a run in the top of the first inning to provide Bearden with a narrow margin to work on. But the Red Sox tied it up in the bottom of the first.

The tie endured for two innings. But in the fourth Cleveland rallied for four runs and picked up a single counter in the fifth to make the score Cleveland 6, Boston 1. In the last half of the sixth Bearden got into a little trouble, allowing two runs—but they were the last two runs the Red Sox were able to score. Bearden shut them out in the last three innings, and Cleveland went on to win, 8-3. Two of the three runs scored on Bearden were unearned.

The Cleveland clubhouse was jubilant after the victory, and everyone on the team wanted to shake Bearden's hand. It was a heady moment for Bearden, but a sobering one too. For now they were in the World Series against the Boston Braves, and this was a new and even bigger challenge. He knew he would get to start a game in the Series and that it would be the biggest game of his career. It was one he had to win, because it would mean that he had traveled a painful path from a serious war casualty to a World Series winner!

That, he thought, would be going all the way.

The city of Cleveland was agog with the success of their ball team. Clevelanders had waited a long time for a pennant winner. The Indians had not captured the flag in twenty-eight years—a dry spell that had now been quenched by Bearden's play-off victory against the Red Sox. The race had been a tight one, and the finish had been dramatic; Cleveland fans now looked forward to more of the same when the Indians clashed with the Boston Braves in the Fall Classic.

The enthusiasm of the Cleveland fans was given a rude jolt in the first game, however. Bob Feller was selected to pitch against Johnny Sain of the Braves, and Feller pitched a magnificent game. For seven tense innings neither team scored. When the Braves came to bat in the last of the eighth, they had accumulated only one hit off Feller. But Feller got into trouble by walking Bill Salkeld. Mike McCormick sacrificed him to second with a perfect bunt. Unwilling to take a chance with Eddie Stanky, Feller walked him purposely, moving Phil Masi, who was running for Salkeld, to second. He scored minutes later when Tommy Holmes lashed a single to right.

The Indians failed to score in the top of the ninth, and that was the ballgame—Braves 1, Indians 0. Feller had lost a brilliant two-hitter.

It was Bob Lemon's turn in the second game, and he had better luck. He won his game 4-1.

Thankful to have split the first two games in the Braves' ball park, the Indians returned to Cleveland's huge Metropolitan Stadium for the third contest.

It was a dark, dreary day, with rain falling right up to game-time. Neither team could take infield or batting practice, and the monstrous tarpaulins remained on the field until a few minutes before starting time. A light sprinkle was falling when the game started—but there were an incredible

70,306 fans in the stadium to see if the knuckleballing Gene
Bearden could put the Indians a game up in the series.

When Bearden warmed up for the game, he sensed that this
was a day when he would have his stuff. *If we can get one run,*
he thought, *just one run, we'll win. I think I can shut these guys
out.*

In the first inning Bearden got the Braves out in order. In the
second Frank McCormick singled with one out, but Bearden
got the next two batters easily. Clint Conatser topped a knuckler, and the aluminum plate in Bearden's leg didn't prevent
him from leaping off the mound and pouncing on the ball like
a cat to throw the runner out at first. Then he got Phil Masi on
an easy pop-up.

In the third Eddie Stanky opened with a single and Vernon
Bickford, the Braves' pitcher, bunted him to second. But
Bearden closed the gates on the rally. He grabbed Tommy
Holmes's bounder to the mound and threw him out, and then
induced shortstop Alvin Dark to hit a soft liner to Walt Jud-
nich in short right field.

Meanwhile, Cleveland had done nothing with the slants of
Bickford, but in the bottom of the third they created a few
fireworks. After catcher Jim Hegan opened the inning by foul-
ing out, Bearden strode to the plate. Bickford figured he could
overpower the Cleveland pitcher and threw a blazing fastball,
high and hard. Bearden swung and felt the satisfying shock
of a well-hit ball travel up the bat into his forearms. The ball
carried on a line against the fence in right field at the 320-
foot mark, and Bearden raced into second with a double.

Bickford was noticeably upset by this turn of events, and
before he could get himself straightened out he had walked
Dale Mitchell. Two men on, one man out.

Outfielder Larry Doby was now the batter. Bickford worked

carefully on him and finally induced him to hit a ground ball to Eddie Stanky at second. It was a ready-made double play, and Stanky shoveled it expertly to shortstop Alvin Dark covering second. But then things went wrong. Dark, trying to complete a fast double play to get the Braves out of the inning, threw the ball past first baseman Frank McCormick. Bearden raced around third and scored to put the Indians ahead, 1-0.

It was at this time that the sun broke through the clouds and brightened the ball park—like a ray of hope from the heavens for Gene Bearden. Now he had his run, and he went to work on the Braves in the fourth with renewed vigor. Mike McCormick lined a single to the outfield to lead off and Bearden said to himself: *That's all. Gotta shut the door again.* Bob Elliott, a husky long-ball hitter, was next up, and Bearden knuckleballed him until he lifted a fly ball to Doby. Then Frank McCormick topped a knuckler and hit it back to Bearden. Gene whipped it to Joe Gordon for the put-out at second, and Gordon nailed McCormick at first for a double play.

Cleveland stretched its lead in the last of the fourth. Bickford walked Ken Keltner, first man up for the Indians, and then struck out Walt Judnich. But Eddie Robinson drilled a sharp line single to left, sending Keltner to second. When Jim Hegan also singled, Keltner raced home with the second Indian run. Bearden got his second hit, a single, and Bickford was taken out of the game. His reliefer got the side out without further scoring.

The score at the end of the fourth: Cleveland 2, Boston 0.

That was the way the score stayed. The Braves managed only two more hits off Bearden—a double by Dark in the sixth and a single by Elliott in the seventh. Bearden put them down one-two-three in the eighth and ninth.

The 2-0 victory put the Indians one game ahead in the World Series, and the accolades that came Bearden's way were overwhelming. Actually, the game has gone down in baseball history as a classic pitching performance—and a look at the statistics will tell you why.

Not only had Gene Bearden pitched a five-hit shutout against the Braves, he had taken only eighty-four pitches to do it. Of those eighty-four pitches, fifty-six were strikes. Of the five hits off him, four were singles, and all day long Bearden's baffling knuckleball had the Boston batters hitting the ball into the ground. Only four fly balls were hit to the outfield.

In Bearden's last three starts—the key game against the Detroit Tigers, the playoff game with the Red Sox and the World Series game with the Braves—the flutterball specialist had allowed only one earned run in twenty-seven innings!

That game could have been a fitting climax to the Gene Bearden story, but there was more to come. Bearden had a hand in the final game too!

Following Cleveland's 2-0 victory, the Indians went on to grab the next game, 2-1. That gave them a 3-1 lead in games over the Braves. But the Braves bounced back to take the next game, 11-5, closing the gap to Cleveland 3 games, Boston 2.

In the sixth game the Indians started Bob Lemon in an effort to wrap up the Series. Lemon sailed along in reasonably good fashion until he weakened in the eighth. Boudreau had Bearden warming up in the bull pen, ready to use him in a relief role if it became necessary.

With the score 4-2 in Cleveland's favor and a runner on base, Boudreau decided it was time for Bearden to dazzle the opposition with his knuckleball.

Bearden came in from the bull pen and threw his warm-up

pitches. There were two out, and Phil Masi was at the plate. If he could get Masi to end the inning, Bearden was sure he could set the Braves down in the ninth.

But Masi had other ideas. He smashed Bearden's first pitch against the wall for a double, and the score became Indians 4, Boston Braves 3.

But Bearden proved adequate for the job at hand. He got the next batter and then mowed down three in a row in the Braves' ninth to win the game.

Cleveland had won its first World Series in twenty-eight years, and much of the credit for the victory belonged to Bearden. He had pitched the game that placed them in a tie for the league lead, had then won the play-off game, had hurled a shutout in the third game of the World Series and had saved the last game to wrap it up.

The young man who doctors five years before had said "would not amount to much if he lived" had amounted to a great deal in winning the pennant and the World Series for the Cleveland Indians.

2

Pete Gray...
case of the one-armed outfielder

The history of major-league baseball is studded with the names of ballplayers who performed in the big time for just one year, or even less, and then faded from sight. These were players who obviously did not have the talent to play in the majors. Somewhere along the line scouts had seen them play, had noticed a tiny spark of talent that they hoped might leap into flame on a big-league diamond and had signed them to a contract. When they failed to live up to the scouts' vague expectations, they rapidly slipped out of the majors into oblivion.

For the most part these players were mistakes—errors in judgment by scouts and big-league clubs—and should never have trodden on a major-league diamond at all.

However, there is one man who played for only a single season in the major leagues who belongs in a class by himself. He is Pete Gray, an outfielder for the old St. Louis Browns in 1945, who played in seventy-seven games, batted .218 and then disappeared from baseball. And if you think that is not much of a record, you are right—except for one very important thing.

Pete Gray had only one arm.

Pete Gray, of Lithuanian extraction, was born Peter J. Wyshner on March 6, 1917, in the coal-mining town of Nanticoke, Pennsylvania. His father was a coal miner who worked long hours in black, sooty corridors drilled into the Pennsylvania earth, and when he returned home to his wife and five children at the close of day his face was etched not only with coal dust but with the weariness of a day's hard labor. He earned very little money at this occupation, and young Pete learned early that without money you could be hungry, cold and miserable.

At the age of six, Pete had already made up his mind that he would, somehow, make enough money when he grew up to buy a nice home for whatever family he might have. He did not know just how he would go about this, but he was already fond of playing baseball and he thought that perhaps baseball would be the means by which he would earn his livelihood.

The idea appealed strongly to Pete. Wouldn't it be great, he thought, if he could someday play in the major leagues? His mind danced with extravagant dreams of accomplishment— how he would scamper over the well-manicured big-league diamonds, how he would hit a home run into the far confines of the bleachers, how he would make dazzling catches against outfield walls and screens and how he would play in Yankee Stadium and hear the roar of a big New York crowd ring in his ears. It was heady stuff for a six-year-old—so exciting that it seemed real to him, something that was bound to happen, something he would make happen.

But then tragedy struck, and the dream splintered into little pieces and crashed around him. Returning from a day of baseball with other boys his age, Pete decided to hitch a ride on the back of a car that was going down the bumpy road which passed his house. It was a bad mistake. As he attempted to get a grip on the back of the car, the vehicle suddenly lurched crazily over a rut in the road. Pete was thrown off, and his right arm was caught in the wheel. The arm was so mangled that doctors had to cut it off above the elbow—and with the removal of his arm went Pete's dream of becoming a ballplayer.

Pete spent the following year between the hospital and his home. When the savage wound of the amputation healed, he found that he had to relearn many things. He had to learn how to dress himself without the use of his right arm, to eat his meals one-handed, to redo all the things he had always done so easily before. Learning these things was difficult at first, but he mastered them—and with his success Pete began to hope again for a baseball career. If he could relearn other things, then why couldn't he learn to play baseball with one arm? The thought excited him. He *would* play baseball again! He was sure of it!

Pete decided that the first thing he had to do was learn how to swing a bat with one arm. He perfected this maneuver by tossing stones in the air and hitting them with a bat. As he improved his left-handed swing, he found he could drive the stones farther and farther and even control the direction in which he drove them, pulling them to "right field" or slicing them to "left." In time he grew so proficient at hitting one-handed—not to mention catching—that he became a permanent member of the local semi-pro Hanover Pitt club. Not only that, he became one of the stars of the team, and Hanover Pitt began to draw larger crowds than it had ever attracted before —most of the spectators coming to see the miraculous play of Peter J. Wyshner, who had now assumed the shorter name of Pete Gray.

Pete's success as a semi-pro spurred his ambition to become a major-leaguer. He refused to concede that playing major-league ball with one arm was impossible, although most of the people who watched him doubted his ability to ever play in the big time. Sure, he was doing well as a semi-pro, and more power to him. But climb the ladder to the top? Up through the various echelons of minor-league ball to the major leagues? With one arm? Impossible!

Pete didn't think so, however, and one day he fired off a letter to Mel Ott, manager of the New York Giants, asking for a tryout. Ott invited him to come down to the Giants' training camp in Miami, but when the amazed Ott saw that he had only one arm, he shook his head sadly. "I'm sorry, kid," he said. "But it's tough enough for a man with two arms to play major-league ball."

On another occasion he contacted Connie Mack, venerable old manager of the Philadelphia Athletics, but Mack's reaction was the same. In neither case did he receive a tryout, only regrets.

Still Pete would not quit. Early in the 1940s he went to New York and played semi-pro baseball with the Bay Parkways team in Brooklyn, figuring that, if he played in New York, there was a greater possibility of a scout discovering him.

It was not until 1943, though, that Pete received his first big break. A scout for the Three Rivers club of Quebec in the Canadian-American League saw him play and, since Three Rivers was practically panting for talent at the time, he sent a glowing telegram to the manager. Pete was invited to come to Quebec, and when Pete showed up the manager was astounded. The scout had said nothing about Pete's missing arm!

This time, however, the desperate manager decided to try

Pete Gray in the outfield. Pete lost no time getting started. In his first time at bat, he hit a home run with the bases loaded— and he was on his way. That year he batted an amazing .381 to lead the league in hitting, and his performance won him a contract with the Memphis Chicks in the Southern Association the following season.

The Southern Association was a fast league, a real test for any aspiring young player. For a man with one arm it was a test of utmost cruelty. Those who had been following Pete Gray's career with some skepticism felt that this time he had reached out too far. This was where Pete would have to come to grips with reality, would have to recognize that there was a limitation to what a one-armed man could do in the intricate and demanding game of baseball. This, they said, would be his cruel moment of truth.

So what did Pete Gray do? He simply batted .333 for the Chicks, led the league with sixty-eight stolen bases, cracked five home runs, fielded flawlessly, provided the spark that drove the team to the championship and was voted the league's Most Valuable Player!

This was an amazing record that was envied by every two-armed man in the league, and Pete began to get requests from people he had never heard of to make personal appearances. The offers angered him. Each one seemed to indicate that the sender regarded him as an oddity. One man offered him considerable money to put on an exhibition, and he wired back a curt reply: "Thank you for the offer but I am a ballplayer, not an exhibitionist." Another promoter wanted him to make a half-hour appearance, demonstrating how he caught and batted a ball. He sent the man a wire that said, "I would gladly play in a game. I am not a freak."

And certainly he was not. With his great season as a member of the Chicks, Pete Gray had proved, to himself and others, that it was entirely possible to overcome the handicap of a missing arm and play baseball in fast company. He had climbed the difficult baseball ladder and was now perched on one of the topmost rungs. Would his performance in the Southern Association earn him a promotion to a big-league club?

It did. The St. Louis Browns signed him—and Pete Gray was suddenly in the major leagues!

It must be admitted that there were two reasons why the Browns decided to sign Pete Gray. One was obviously his fine record with the Chicks, which told them that he would be able to help the club in the pennant race. The other was that World War II was in progress and many established stars were in the service, and all teams were scratching for players. Baseball was at low ebb, and teams were made up of youngsters who had not yet been drafted into service, old veterans who were too old for the draft and those classified 4-F because of ill health or physical defects. Even under such circumstances a one-armed ballplayer was a tremendous gamble—but the Browns couldn't overlook Pete Gray's great minor-league record. They simply had to give him a chance.

Pete knew all this, and he knew, too, that the chips were really down this time. But he was still confident and determined to succeed, and in spring training with the Browns, he applied himself diligently. He hustled with the enthusiasm of any rookie wanting to make it in the big leagues, and Luke Sewell, manager of the St. Louis Browns, spent half of spring training shaking his head in amazement at Pete's exploits on the field.

When reporters asked Pete questions about whether or not he thought he could make the grade with the Browns, he always hedged. "I don't know," he'd say. "I don't know if I can play with the big players." But then he would trot out on the field and do everything the "big players" were doing, and do it just as well.

Pete made the team, all right, and when the Browns played in St. Louis the fans swarmed into the ball park to see him. He quickly became the idol of the crowd. His batting technique and his skill in the outfield had been honed to a fine edge, and the fans could do nothing but marvel at his accomplishments.

When he batted, he would stand in the left-handed batter's box and grip the bat with his one hand, choking it just a little to better control it. Cocking the bat over his left shoulder, he would wait for the pitch and then swing. Some players lack bat control when they use both hands; Pete managed it with one. His swing was level and almost always got a piece of the ball. He struck out no oftener than most players, and he got a reasonable share of hits.

His fielding and throwing were a vision to watch. When a high fly was hit to him, he would settle under the ball, spearing it expertly with his gloved left hand. Then he would toss the ball gently in the air—no more than six inches, which was enough for him to flip off his loose-fitting glove. He would catch the ball again in his bare hand and whip it back to the infield. And, remarkably, all this was done in a mere twinkle of time. On hits to his field, Pete handled the ball with the same expertness, and opposing runners soon learned that the second or two's delay caused by Pete's flipping off his glove and throwing was rarely enough to permit them to take an extra base.

On top of all this, Pete Gray was a hustling ballplayer. He

ran the bases with great speed, chased after flies and ground balls with complete abandon. He never slowed down, and he made every play an all-out effort.

For all this, the St. Louis fans loved him. He was the people's choice, the one guy they paid their money to see, the man in the lineup who could excite them. They applauded every move he made. If he committed an error or struck out— so what? The fans cheered him anyway.

Pete had many memorable moments with the Browns, but it was probably in a game with the old Philadelphia Athletics that Pete won the undying affection of every fan in St. Louis. It was late in the game, and the score was tied. The Browns had a runner on second, which meant little because the Browns had demonstrated a talent for leaving base-runners stranded. Pete walked up to the plate and calmly one-armed a smash off the wall for a double to bring in the winning run. That night St. Louis would have gladly given Pete Gray the City Hall.

But the glory days were short for Pete. Before the 1946 season began, the Browns released him. World War II was over, and the veteran players were returning. Baseball is not a game in which sentiment abounds, and there was no longer any room for a one-armed player on any major-league roster. The Browns let their one-armed marvel go.

Pete Gray faded from baseball then, but he had realized an impossible dream. He had played in the major leagues—the only one-armed man ever to do so—and had etched his name indelibly in the record books for all time.

It was a triumph of courage such as baseball had never before seen—and has not seen since.

3

Mickey Mantle . . .
the man who played with pain

He sat on a small stool in front of the open-faced locker where his baseball uniform hung, a big man with broad shoulders and the unmistakable physique of a powerful athlete. Rolls of bandage and tape lay at his feet.

The big man was in obvious pain as he carefully wrapped the bandage around his right knee, then repeated the operation on his left. Before he was finished, he had bandaged and taped both legs, from the hip almost to the ankle, wincing as he went through what had become a daily ordeal.

Slowly he rose from his stool, weariness in his manner, and took a stiff-legged step toward the locker. With some difficulty he got into his trousers and shirt, then put the spiked shoes on his feet. Slowly, as if every step had to be taken with extreme care, he hobbled down the runway between the clubhouse and the field.

Mickey Mantle was ready to play another ballgame.

There is probably no more inspiring story in baseball than that of Mickey Mantle, the gritty outfielder of the New York Yankees whose pain-filled but illustrious career spanned almost two decades. This remarkable player not only suffered an injury during his boyhood that would have stopped most young men from seeking a career in baseball, but played during much of his major-league career with pain as a companion.

Mickey Charles Mantle was born on October 20, 1931, in Spavinaw, Oklahoma. If ever a boy was destined to become a ballplayer, it was Mickey. His father, Elvin (Mutt) Mantle, was a lead and zinc miner, and he was determined that his boy would have a better life than he had lived. Both the elder Mantle and his father, Charles, had been semi-pro ballplayers around Oklahoma, and it was therefore natural that Mickey's father decided early that the road to a better life for his son was through baseball.

The elder Mantle named his boy Mickey, after the great Philadelphia and Detroit catcher Mickey Cochrane (although Cochrane's true first name was Gordon). When Mickey reached the ripe old age of five years, his father began to teach him how to play baseball. A naturally right-handed hitter, young Mickey was quickly converted into a switch hitter. With some insistent coaching from his father, it was not long before Mickey learned to bat from either side of the plate.

Despite this early training, Mickey decided to participate in other sports—namely, basketball and football—when he entered Commerce High School in Commerce, Oklahoma. As a basketball player he was the fastest man on the court, and he helped Commerce High set a fantastic record of 120 wins against only six losses in three years. But it was in football that he almost met his Waterloo. One day, in a game, he was kicked in the left shin. It was only a bruise, and he brushed it off. But when the leg began to swell and turn a purplish color, his father took him to a hospital in Oklahoma City for an examination. Tests revealed that Mickey had osteomyelitis, a bone disease that could be controlled but never cured.

The news hit the Mantle family like a thunderclap. Mickey's father envisioned all his dreams going up in smoke. How could his son become a great ballplayer with a chronic bone disease? It seemed that all his plans for Mickey had been cruelly destroyed.

Mickey was on crutches for several months, but he finally was able to cast them aside and play baseball for the high school team. He immediately showed a greater capacity for baseball than other sports, and the bone problem did not seem to bother him much. Mickey's father was delighted, to say the least, and he began to believe that maybe his dreams would come true after all. Perhaps, despite everything, his son would become a major-leaguer.

One day Tom Greenwade, a New York Yankee scout with a sharp eye for baseball talent, saw Mickey Mantle playing shortstop for his high school team. He watched him as he hit from both sides of the plate, and took note of his even swing, the way he handled himself in the field and the natural baseball instinct he seemed to have. He waited patiently until Mickey graduated from high school and then signed him for $1,500. Those were pre-bonus days, and Mickey signed gladly. The Yankees sent him to their Class D farm club at Independence, Missouri, hoping that he would develop in time to take over the shortstop position with the Yankees when the aging Phil Rizzuto was through.

Mickey batted a highly acceptable .313 with Independence and earned a promotion the following year to Joplin in the Class C Western Association. All he did at Joplin was lead the league in batting with .383, in runs scored with 141 and in hits with 199. Among those hits were 26 home runs, 12 triples and 30 doubles. He also drove in 136 runs.

Only one questionable mark appeared on his record, and it was a serious one. He made 55 errors!

Nevertheless, in the spring of 1951 he was asked to report to the Yankees' spring training camp at Phoenix, Arizona. Mickey was excited and thrilled. It was his big opportunity, and he made the most of it. He hit with lusty power from both sides of the plate and impressed everyone, including manager Casey Stengel, with the vicious liners he hit to all fields and into the stands. But the error problem persisted. His glove work was not the best, and Stengel was convinced that Mantle had no chance to take over Phil Rizzuto's job at the vital shortstop position.

Where, then, could they play a guy who could murder the ball but not necessarily catch it? Stengel brooded over this question all through spring training and didn't make his decision until the team was on the way north to open the American League season.

"He'll play right field," Ole Case finally announced.

The decision was not marked with genius. In the first game he played, Mantle got a single; he hit his first major-league home run on May 1—a prodigious drive into the right-field seats off Randy Gumpert of Chicago. But his fielding was still erratic, and the front office, if not Stengel himself, began to wonder if another year in the minors might not correct his fielding deficiencies. Finally, the Yanks—a team with a good chance to win the pennant—decided they could no longer gamble on Mickey. In early July, Mantle was sent to Kansas City, then in the American Association, for more seasoning.

Mantle was depressed by his return to the minors, but he

knew he had to do the best job possible with the Kansas City Blues if he hoped to return to the Yankee lineup. So what did he do? He simply hit .361 for the Blues and, unable to resist this kind of hitting, the Yankees decided to bring him back. Mantle finished out the 1951 season in a Yankee uniform, and when New York won the pennant that year, Mickey suddenly found himself facing the New York Giants in a World Series.

But the glory of playing right field for the Yankees in the Fall Classic was short-lived for Mantle. It ended in the second game, while his father watched from the stands.

Willie Mays, a sterling young outfielder in his first year with the Giants, hit a long fly to right-center. Mantle raced for the ball as center-fielder Joe DiMaggio cut across from center. Mantle had a lead on the ball when all at once he felt a sharp pain in his right knee. Joe DiMaggio made the catch as Mantle collapsed to the ground, writhing in pain. At the hospital the injury was diagnosed as a torn ligament, and Mantle was through for the season.

During the off-season the injury mended, but the Mantle family was struck by another tragedy. Mickey's father died of cancer. He had, at least, realized his ambition by seeing his son play major-league baseball before he passed away.

Mickey Mantle went to spring training camp in 1952 determined to put a lock on the center-field job with the Yankees. Joe DiMaggio had completed his illustrious career with New York, and the center-field position was up for grabs. Mantle worked hard on the area that needed improvement—his fielding. Casey Stengel watched him closely and noted that Mantle's fielding skills had, indeed, improved. When the team opened the 1952 season, Mickey Mantle was the successor to the great DiMaggio in center field.

From that time until the end of his career, in 1968, nobody was able to take the job away from him. In 1952 he hit .311 with 171 hits in 549 at-bats, collected 23 home runs and drove in 50. The Yankees won the pennant again and took on the Brooklyn Dodgers in the World Series. The Dodgers battled the Yanks for seven games, but the New Yorkers finally won. Mantle contributed in a big way to the Yankee victory. His home run in the eighth inning of the sixth game, when the Yanks were down three games to two, enabled the New Yorkers to win 3-2, and his homer in the sixth inning of the seventh game represented the go-ahead run in the Yankees' final 4-2 win.

Mickey Mantle's career was off to a rousing start, and what a career it became! It was measured not only in the hits and home runs he got, not only in the great fielding plays he made, not only in the games he won singlehandedly, but also in his courage—the stamina and grit that made him play most of his long career with injuries and pain that would have sidelined any other ballplayer.

Over the next dozen years he became not only the greatest player on the Yankee team, but one of the greatest in baseball. His batting skills were without peer. In 1953 he batted .295 (almost a bad year for him), and then for the next five years hit .300, .306, .353, .365 and .304. Home runs boomed from his bat in clusters—37 in 1955 and 52 in 1956, when he won the Triple Crown with 130 RBIs and a .353 batting average. In 1961 he took aim at Ruth's record, this time hitting 54 round-trippers and batting .317 for the season. In the thirteen years from 1952 through 1964 he hit .300 or better ten times.

But the most sensational feature of Mantle's eighteen-year career was his awesome power. He hit home runs for such distances that they began to tape-measure them—565 feet at Washington, 550 feet in Chicago. Around this powerful young man the Yankees built a dynasty, winning eleven pennants and six World Series during his peak years.

But none of it came easy to Mickey. All through these great years he played with more than his share of injuries—bruises, fractures, pulled muscles—but he would not permit them to discourage him or allow them to permanently damage his career. As long as he was able to hobble onto the field, Mickey Mantle played baseball. As he once said, "It's the only thing I know. What else can I do?"

An example of his dedication to the game occurred late in the 1961 season. This was the year when he and his teammate Roger Maris were both threatening Babe Ruth's home run record of 60 in a season. Late in the year, when Mantle had built his home run total to 53 as against Maris's 56, Mickey was hit by a virus and placed in the hospital. The inactivity galled him. Five days later he returned to the lineup and, in a weakened condition, hit his 54th homer. The next day he was back in the hospital again as Maris went on to break Ruth's record by hitting his 61st round-tripper.

During his hospitalization, Mantle developed an abscess on his hip and was in considerable pain. But when the Yankees prepared to meet the Cincinnati Reds in the World Series, he left the hospital and said to Ralph Houk, the Yankee manager, "I'm ready to play." Houk, realizing that Mickey was still weak, held him out of the first two games, but allowed him to play in the third. Mantle played the entire game despite excruciating pain, but in the fourth game he lasted only four innings. The abscess began to bleed and, when he ran out a single in the fourth inning, Houk noticed that blood had soaked through his pants and formed an ugly red stain. Amazed, Houk immediately took him out of the game and sent in a pinch runner.

"I didn't know how badly he was hurting," Houk said later. "He never mentioned the abscess. He was out there doing his best when nine out of ten players would have been flat on their backs in bed."

Mantle's refusal to quit was a measure of the courage he brought to the game of baseball.

During the winter season Mantle's health improved, and when the 1962 season got under way he was at the peak of his form. Everyone could see that a great season was ahead for the big slugger from Oklahoma. He got away to a flying start, but it didn't last long. On May 18 disaster struck. It struck viciously and without warning—at a time when Mickey was hitting .315, with seven home runs and seventeen RBIs.

New York was playing the Minnesota Twins at Yankee Stadium that night. When they came to bat in the last half of the ninth inning, Minnesota held a 4-3 lead. Mantle came up to the plate in the critical inning with a man on second and two out.

Sam Mele, manager of the Twins, called Dick Stigman from the bull pen to pitch to Mantle. "Curveball him low," was his instruction to the reliefer. "Don't give him anything good. Walk him if you have to."

Stigman threw Mantle a curveball, all right, but he got it high instead of low. Mantle hit a hot shot between third and short that looked like a sure hit.

As he raced for first base, Mantle saw the Minnesota shortstop, Zoilo Versalles, go into the hole and glove the ball. A long and accurate throw to first was needed to retire Mantle, and Mickey knew he had a good chance of beating the play.

He put on a burst of speed, straining for the bag—and then, suddenly, there was a stabbing pain in his right thigh and he crumpled to the ground a few feet from the bag. As he went down he felt a tearing pain in his left knee, too. *I've hurt myself again,* was all he could think.

A sickening moan escaped the spectators in the stands when Mantle failed to get to his feet. He lay awkwardly on the grassy infield, twisting in pain, and manager Houk and the trainer rushed to his aid. A quick examination convinced them that Mantle was badly hurt, and they called for the stretcher. But Mickey would have none of that. With the help of a team-mate and a coach, he got to his feet and was half-carried from the field. In the clubhouse he was given a pair of crutches, and he stood there in the middle of the locker-lined room and said, "I'll be out a week. No longer than that."

He was out for almost five weeks.

What Mantle's absence from the lineup did to the Yankees' pennant chances is difficult to estimate, but there is no doubt that it hurt them severely. Playing only .500 ball during Mantle's absence turned what had started out as a walk-away to the pennant into a serious dogfight between New York, Minnesota and Los Angeles.

Sitting on the bench frustrated Mantle. Mickey hated to miss the action. He resented taking even a one-day rest. "If you start sitting them out," he said, "first thing you know you're sitting them all out. And I don't want to be a guy who just sits around."

Despite his eagerness to get back into action, Mantle was unable to return to the lineup until June 16 in Cleveland. It was the eighth inning; the Yankees were behind, 7-6, and had two men on base. Houk looked at Mantle.

"Can you pinch-hit?" he asked.

Mantle got up without a word and went to the bat rack.

"If you hit into a double play," Houk said, "don't try to beat the throw to first. Give up on it."

Mantle made sure he wouldn't have to run fast. Even though he had not batted for almost five weeks, Mickey hit a three-run homer into the stands.

Before the 1962 season ended, Mantle suffered still another major injury. This one occurred on September 4—a pulled muscle in his side—and again the Yankees stumbled during his absence. For a while it looked as if either Minnesota or Los Angeles would steal the pennant, but Mantle returned to the Yankee lineup just in time to rescue the New Yorkers. In his first game he hit a home run to defeat the Tigers, went three-for-five in the next game to lead the Yankees to another victory and followed with a home run and three RBIs in his third game to propel the Yankees to another pennant.

This time Mantle played the full seven games in the World Series against the San Francisco Giants, and the Yankees won four games to three.

The 1963 season was almost a total loss to Mickey. He got away to another fast start and then, on June 5, he crashed into a fence in Baltimore and broke his foot. He missed a month of action this time, and when he returned he experienced a recurring problem with his left knee, injured the year before, and was of little use to the team the rest of the way.

In 1964 Mantle was healthier than he had been in a long time. He missed only nineteen games and had a good season, batting .303, driving in 111 runs, hitting 35 homers and leading the Yankees to still another pennant. In the World Series against the St. Louis Cardinals, he hit his sixteenth home run to break Babe Ruth's World Series record.

But that year was really the last big one for Mickey Mantle.

His body had taken all the punishment it could endure. It became almost impossible for him to run, and he winced with pain when he swung at a pitch. Still, he tried to play for four more years.

He never again batted .300, and when he retired from the game after the 1968 season he left a statistical legacy for future Yankees to shoot at. He finished eighteen years with a lifetime batting average of .298 (only because he failed to hit .300 in his fading pain-filled years), a total of 536 home runs and 1,509 runs batted in—despite the fact that he missed more than 300 games (equivalent to two seasons) with injuries.

But statistics are bleak figures on a page, and they do not tell the whole story. They do not mention that Mickey Mantle compiled his impressive lifetime record while playing a good part of the time with pain. They do not reveal the courage of the man who put those figures in the record books—how he made the major leagues despite an attack of boyhood osteomyelitis that might have nipped his career in the bud, how he had conquered pain and disaster time after time and still remained the big man of the Yankee team.

Billy Martin, a teammate of Mantle's for six years, put it well. "He played a lot of times when an average guy would have stayed on the bench. He paid a price to be the best, and that's why he became the best."

Even Casey Stengel dropped his usual confused Stengelese and made simple sense when he spoke of Mantle.

"He's the only man I ever saw," he said, "who was a cripple and could outdo the world."

In the athletic sense, Mickey Mantle *was* a cripple. But he wasn't a quitter.

4
Jackie Robinson ...
the man who broke the color barrier

Quite a few athletes have overcome difficult handicaps to star at their chosen sport. Some were considered too small to compete in professional sports. Others had physical ailments or deformities that threatened to keep them forever sidelined. Still others recovered from career-wrecking injuries and went on to greatness.

But Jackie Robinson, the great infielder of the Brooklyn Dodgers from 1947 through 1956, was different. He was big enough, standing five feet, eleven and a half and weighing 195 pounds. He had no physical shortcomings, nor did injuries stand in his way. And as for talent, he had it all—he could hit, throw, run and field better than most players in the league. Only one problem—a monstrous one—stood in the way of his becoming a major-league ballplayer.

He was black.

Today, major-league baseball has many black players, and a great number of them are outstanding stars. The names come to mind easily—Hank Aaron, Willie Mays, Frank Robinson, Roberto Clemente, Maury Wills, Willie Horton, Richie Allen, Tony Oliva. But prior to 1947 there were no black players at all in the major leagues. Jackie Robinson was the first—and because he was the first he had the tough, almost impossible job of blazing a trail for all other blacks who would follow him.

His was a psychological handicap, one that in the 1940s seemed impossible for any lone man to overcome.

Jack Roosevelt Robinson was born on January 31, 1919, in Cairo, Georgia. His parents were sharecroppers, tenant farmers who paid their rent with a share of the crops they raised. A few years after young Jackie was born, his family moved to Pasadena, California, and as a growing boy he sold newspapers to help support the family.

Jackie was interested in all sports, and when he entered high school he played baseball, football and basketball and participated in track-and-field events. Anxious to get a college education, he entered the University of California at Los Angeles (UCLA) after graduation from high school, but he never finished his schooling there. His education was interrupted when he was drafted into the Army during World War II. By the time he was mustered out of the Army, he had gained the rank of second lieutenant.

Jackie did not return to school after his hitch in the Army. Instead, he joined the Kansas City Monarchs, one of the best Negro baseball teams in the country. He was installed at shortstop and immediately became one of the club's top stars.

In those days, white ballplayers who had dreams of playing some day in the major leagues had some possibility of having the dreams come true. Jackie Robinson had the same dream, but he knew there was little chance for him. No major-league team had ever hired a black player, and there seemed to be an unwritten rule among owners that the major leagues would forever remain white.

But what Jackie Robinson did not know was that one man, in a high front-office position with the Brooklyn Dodgers, also had a dream. He was a white man named Branch Rickey, and he was aware of the terrible struggle a black man had in making himself a success. His dream was to find a black player good enough to play in the major leagues, and to add him to the Brooklyn roster. He wanted to "break the color barrier" and give black men an equal chance to make good with a major-league club.

It would not be an easy thing to do. There was much prejudice against blacks invading the major leagues, and Branch Rickey knew he would never succeed with just an ordinary black player. The man he chose had to be a superior ballplayer, a player so talented that his teammates could not help but accept him. And he had to be a man of strong courage who could stand up under the barrage of taunts and insults that inevitably would be thrown at him from every dugout in the National League.

His man, he finally decided, was Jackie Robinson.

Rickey had been hearing great things about Robinson's sparkling play with the Kansas City Monarchs, and he sent Clyde Sukeforth, a Brooklyn scout, to contact the Negro star. Sukeforth went to Chicago, where the Monarchs were playing the Chicago American Giants at Comiskey Park. Sukeforth introduced himself to Robinson before the game.

"I'm here to see you play," he said. "I'm from the Brooklyn Dodgers."

Curiously, this announcement did not excite Jackie Robinson. Scouts had watched him before, but nothing had ever come of it. This man, he thought, was just another one whose report would be filed away and never found again.

This time, however, the script was changed. After the game, Sukeforth was waiting for Robinson at the locker room door.

"Mr. Rickey would like to see you in Brooklyn," he said simply.

Robinson stared. "You mean—" he began.

"I mean," said Sukeforth, "that Branch Rickey sent me down here to get you."

That was the beginning of Robinson's long road to acceptance as a big-league ballplayer. When he arrived in Brooklyn, Rickey—a man who could be both tough and sensitive —made it clear to Jackie that he wanted him to eventually play for the Brooklyn Dodgers.

"One year in the minors at Montreal," Rickey said, "and you should be ready."

Jackie Robinson could hardly believe that he was actually slated to play with the Dodgers. He wondered if it would work out—a black man on an all-white team.

"It won't be easy," Rickey warned him. "You'll be heckled from the bench. They'll call you every name in the book. The pitchers will throw at your head. They'll make it plain they don't like you, and they'll try to make it so tough that you'll give it all up and quit."

Robinson's lips went tight. "I won't quit," he said.

"That's fine, but you won't fight back either," Rickey said sternly. "You will have to take everything they dish out and never strike back. That's important. Because you are going to have to show them you're not only a ballplayer but a gentleman. And when they finally realize you're both, then they'll accept you." He looked at Robinson from beneath scowling black eyebrows. "Do you have the guts to take it?"

Robinson nodded. He knew he was destined to face the grimmest year or two of his life, but he was ready.

"I can take it, Mr. Rickey," he said.

On October 23, 1945, Branch Rickey officially announced that the Brooklyn Dodgers had signed Jackie Robinson to a contract and assigned him to play with the Montreal Royals in the International League. The unexpected announcement received a mixed reaction. Some farsighted people were in favor of blacks playing in the higher echelons of baseball; others were hostile and bitter. Even those in favor, however, expressed doubt that it would work. The sports editor of the New York *Daily News* put it bluntly: "Robinson will not make the grade in the big league this year or next. He is a 1000-to-1 shot."

It didn't take long for the bigots to react to the appearance of Robinson on a baseball field occupied by white players. The Montreal team held spring training at Daytona Beach, Florida, but they allowed early comers to take drills at a nearby camp in Sanford. Jackie worked out for just two days in Sanford, and then the ax fell. Sanford's prejudiced civic leaders demanded that he get out of town.

The insolent demand infuriated Robinson, but he remembered Branch Rickey's words: *You will have to take everything they dish out and never strike back.* Without a word, he left town.

Two weeks later, another difficult situation arose. The Royals had an exhibition game scheduled with the Jacksonville team. When the team arrived at the Jacksonville park, they found the gate padlocked. The game had been called off because Robinson was on the team!

But it was when the Royals met Indianapolis in a spring training game at De Land, Florida, that Jackie suffered his most embarrassing moment. In the first inning Robinson tried to score from second base on a hit. He had to slide home to make it, stirring up a cloud of dust in the process. As the umpire called him safe, Jackie looked up through the dust to see a white policeman standing over him. The policeman had run onto the field and stood scowling down at him.

"Get off the field right now," he snarled, "or I'm putting you in jail!"

Clay Hopper, the Montreal manager, came bounding from the dugout.

"What's going on?" he demanded.

The policeman looked at him coldly. "We ain't havin' Nigras mix with white boys in this town," he said. "Now you tell that Nigra I said to git!"

Again, without a word, Robinson left.

Despite such unpleasant moments, Jackie Robinson established himself as Montreal's second baseman before spring training ended. Most of his teammates had by this time accepted him and recognized him as a talented ballplayer. But there were a few who would not. Robinson was aware of the resentment these few players had for him, and he knew he would simply have to overcome this dislike by his play on the field. He could do it by becoming the best second baseman Montreal had ever seen. That was his goal, his way of fighting back.

The Montreal Royals opened their season against Jersey City, and some 35,000 people were in the stands at Roosevelt Stadium. Jackie was understandably nervous in his first time at bat, and he grounded weakly to the infield. But on his second trip to the plate he hit a line drive into the left-field seats, and the crowd applauded him as he circled the bases.

His first hit for Montreal had been a home run, and the

people in the stands had reacted warmly. Maybe, now that he had left the South, he would gain acceptance after all.

But acceptance did not come easily. Robinson found that rival players were violently hostile. As Branch Rickey had predicted, opposing pitchers threw at him continually, and time after time Jackie hit the dirt, got up, brushed himself off and said nothing. He was constantly insulted from the dugouts by opposing players who called him vile names that were unprintable—but he said nothing. One time in Syracuse a rival player held up a black cat and shouted, "Hey, Robinson! Here's one of your relatives!" Again, Jackie said nothing.

Once, during this trying season, Branch Rickey went to Montreal to talk to Robinson. "As long as you are in baseball," he told Jackie, "you will have to conduct yourself as you are doing now. That is the cross you must bear."

Robinson agreed. He was determined to take it all and fight back only on the diamond with base hits, stolen bases and great fielding plays.

He did this so well that he helped the Montreal Royals win the International League pennant and the Little World Series in 1946. Jackie was the batting champion, with a .349 average, and was named Rookie of the Year. His performance made him a sure bet to be with the Brooklyn Dodgers the following year. And that, he thought, might be even tougher.

Branch Rickey knew that Robinson's promotion to a major-league club was bound to create some problems, and he wanted to make this transition as easy as possible. All through the winter Rickey met with Negro leaders of the community. He told them frankly that they were as much on trial as Jackie Robinson was, and that they would have to see to it that no friction between blacks and whites took place in the stands while Robinson was on the field. The black groups, thankful for what Rickey was doing for a member of their race, promised to cooperate.

With this assured, Rickey then decided to have both the Brooklyn Dodgers and the Montreal Royals hold 1947 spring training in Havana, Cuba. Rickey's reasons were sound. In Havana, Robinson would not be exposed to the racial tensions that existed in America's Southern states. Neither would the Brooklyn players be confronted with Robinson's presence suddenly. He planned to have Robinson continue with the Montreal Royals for most of spring training, so that the Dodger players could see how fine a ballplayer he was. Then, when he announced that Robinson would be promoted to the Brooklyn club, their respect would be such that there should be little resistance.

The first part of Rickey's plan—training in Havana—worked well. But when he announced that Robinson would play first base for Brooklyn (Eddie Stanky was a solid fixture at second base), the protests started. Some of the players took the news without complaint, but a dissident group signed a petition announcing that they would not play with a black player. Rickey called the protesting players into his office and told them bluntly that Robinson would play with the Dodgers whether they liked it or not. Some backed down and agreed to play. Others asked to be traded. Rickey obliged a few of them by shipping them to other clubs, but he was not able to rid himself of all of them.

If the 1946 season with Montreal was a bad dream, the 1947 season with the Dodgers turned out to be a nightmare for Robinson. Everything Branch Rickey had predicted would happen to him did—and more. Pitchers threw at him, making him hit the dirt in almost every game to escape injury. Efforts were made to spike him on the bases. Vicious insults flowed from the dugouts of opposing teams.

Even off the field, Robinson experienced troubles. In some cities where the Dodgers played, Robinson was not allowed to stay in the same hotel with the other players; there were restaurants he was forbidden to enter. But Robinson exhibited a courage few men have been called on to show. He took it all, never losing his temper, never striking back, even though many times he was tempted to hit back with his fists. Jackie Robinson was determined to follow to the letter the instructions of the man who had helped him break into the major leagues.

The hostility toward Jackie Robinson reached a high point on May 6, when the St. Louis Cardinals were scheduled to meet the Brooklyn Dodgers for the first time. A group of Cardinal players decided they would go on strike and refuse to play the game because of Robinson's presence. If that succeeded, they intended to mobilize players on other teams and call a general National League strike.

Fortunately, a sports writer on the New York *Herald-Tribune* exposed the plot against Robinson before it happened, and Ford Frick, then president of the National League, took immediate and bold action. He sent a stinging ultimatum to the players planning to strike.

"If you do this," it warned, "you will be suspended from the league. You will find that the friends you think you have in the press box will not support you, that you will be the outcasts. I do not care if half the league strikes. All will be suspended. This is the United States of America, and one citizen has as much right to play as any other."

The Cardinal players had no recourse but to cancel the strike. But the insults and taunts continued with renewed vigor. One day, when they had reached new heights of viciousness, Pee Wee Reese, the Dodger shortstop who had been born in Ekron, Kentucky, jogged over from his position to talk to

Robinson. He placed his hand gently on Jackie's shoulder as he talked, and a newspaper photographer shot the picture. The photograph appeared in newspapers across the country, and the fact became known that Reese, among all the Dodger players, was the most sympathetic toward Robinson's difficult problem. He saw in Robinson a superb ballplayer, and the color of his face mattered not.

By mid-season there were signs that most of the Dodgers were beginning to accept Robinson on an equal footing. The reason was obvious. Robinson, despite his troubles, was playing spectacular ball, and his play won him the respect that was due him. It required a superman to play good baseball under the tensions that gripped Robinson throughout this critical year, and Jackie proved himself to be a superman. In his first major-league season, he hit .297, batted in 48 runs, collected 12 home runs and stole 29 bases. In the World Series that followed against the New York Yankees, he contributed seven hits in 27 times up for a .259 batting average. And when the season ended, Jackie Robinson was named the National League Rookie of the Year.

In 1948, Eddie Stanky was traded to Boston and Jackie Robinson became the Dodgers' regular second baseman. He found that some of the bitterness of the year before had dissipated, and he felt more at ease on the playing field. That year he virtually duplicated his previous season, batting .296, hitting 12 home runs and increasing his RBIs to 85.

Then came 1949, and Robinson experienced his greatest year in baseball. He won the batting championship with a .342 average, and in the process he collected 16 home runs, drove in 124 and stole 37 bases. His performance led the Dodgers to another pennant, and he was selected as the league's Most Valuable Player.

By 1950 Jackie Robinson had established himself firmly enough in the major leagues that he no longer had to take the insults leveled at him. Branch Rickey agreed that, now, Robinson was free to fight back.

Still, Jackie Robinson did not become too militant, nor did he promiscuously attack other players. He more often answered their taunts with key hits or a stolen base or a great fielding play—the best way to hurt an opponent. But he had his moments against opposing players, umpires and the press —moments when fists were used, or words, or disdainful silence. Still, he never lost the image he had built. He was a great ballplayer and a gentleman—and most people in baseball came to realize this.

Jackie Robinson played ten years for the Brooklyn Dodgers and retired from the game after the 1956 season. He was then thirty-eight years old, and he had set an enviable mark as the first black player in the game. Overcoming one of the greatest handicaps ever to plague a ballplayer, Robinson posted a lifetime batting average of .311 and five years later was elected to baseball's Hall of Fame.

He had not only overcome tremendous odds to shine spectacularly as the first black player in the major leagues, but smoothed the way for other blacks to follow.

Jackie Robinson died of a heart attack on October 24, 1972, at the age of fifty-three. He was eulogized in newspapers across the nation, and baseball—from Commissioner Bowie Kuhn to the lowliest rookie—was saddened. He had earned the tributes paid him by a performance unique in baseball's history, and will not easily be forgotten.

5
Red Schoendienst . . .
from hospital bed to baseball diamond

The redheaded man with the lean, gaunt face sat up in the big hospital bed, bolstered by pillows behind his back. Officials of the Milwaukee Braves had just presented the sick man with a 1959 contract to play baseball, a contract calling for a salary of $35,000. The redheaded man took a pen, signed the contract and smiled.

No one knew if the man in the bed would ever play baseball again—not the man himself, not the baseball officials, not the doctors. Because he had played brilliant major-league baseball for fourteen seasons, the Milwaukee officials felt honor-bound to sign him. But the patient was suffering from tuberculosis, and he was within a month of his thirty-sixth birthday—old for a ballplayer. It looked like the end of the road for him.

The redheaded man was Red Schoendienst.

Albert Fred (Red) Schoendienst never did have the robust physique enjoyed by many athletes. At his prime he stood six feet tall, but he weighed only 165 pounds and his health was fragile. Throughout his career he had been bothered by chest colds, and he had suffered more than his share of injuries. But he had overcome his weight, fragile health and injuries to establish himself as one of the great infielders of the major leagues. Now he had to show that he could overcome the worst calamity that had ever befallen him—a bout with the dreaded TB.

Red Schoendienst was well equipped for the battle, for he had been a creature of misfortune almost since his boyhood. Born February 2, 1923, in Germantown, Illinois, he was one of seven children in the family of Joseph and Mary Schoendienst. His father was a coal miner who struggled to support his family on meager wages and played semi-pro baseball when he had the time and energy to do so.

When Red reached the age of fourteen, he quit New Baden High School to try to help his family financially. The Great Depression was on, and jobs were scarce. As a result, Red was forced to do odd jobs wherever he could find them. He cut lawns and helped nearby farmers in the field. But when he was not working, he occupied himself either by fishing or playing baseball.

Baseball came naturally to Red, and he was usually the star of any kid team formed on the vacant lots of Germantown. He was a naturally right-handed hitter, but because he was so much better than his teammates they forced him to bat left-handed to "even up" the strength of the two teams. Before long, Red could hit equally well from either side of the plate.

In 1939, at the age of sixteen, Red Schoendienst joined the Civilian Conservation Corps, a federal agency created during the Depression that administered projects aimed at conservation of natural resources. He was sent to work at a camp in Greenville, Illinois, and it was while he was at this camp that he suffered a severe eye injury that was to trouble him throughout his career in baseball.

Red was standing near a young worker at the camp who was driving nails in a wood fence. A nail, hit a glancing blow, ricocheted off a fence post and struck Red in the left eye. Doctors examined the injury and announced that there was no hope of saving the eye. They suggested that the best thing he could do would be to have the eye removed.

Fortunately, Red refused, and in the long run the doctors were proved wrong. The eye healed slowly, and Red found that he had some sight left in it. There was enough impairment, however, that the military service temporarily excused him from the World War II draft. Wanting to serve his country in some capacity, Red took a job at Scott Field in Belleville, Illinois, as a civilian supply clerk.

In June, 1942, when Red Schoendienst was nineteen years old, he heard that the St. Louis Cardinals were opening a try-out camp at old Sportsman's Park in St. Louis. Red was convinced there was no better way to make a living than by playing a game he loved, and he reported to the Cardinal camp. Joe Mathes, a Cardinal scout, was impressed enough with Red's talents to sign him to a Class D contract and send him to the Cardinals' farm club at Union City, Tennessee, in the Kitty League.

Red started batting right-handed for Union City, but after a couple of games he realized that his damaged eye gave him a blind spot against curves thrown by right-handers. He reported this to his manager and said, "I think I'll bat left-handed."

The manager looked doubtful. "Who says you can?" he asked.

"I used to do it when I was a kid."

The manager shrugged. "Try it, then."

Red tried it, and it worked. Batting from the left side of the plate, Red found that he had a better look at the ball—and he began hitting with authority.

Red played only a half dozen games at Union City (batting .407) and was transferred to Albany in the Georgia-Florida league. He played most of the 1942 season at second base for Albany, batting .269, and finished the year with nine games at shortstop for Lynchburg in the Piedmont League, hitting the ball at a .472 clip.

This performance earned Red a promotion, and in 1943 he moved up to Rochester, New York, in the faster International League. All he did at Rochester was play second base flawlessly, lead the league with a .337 batting average and earn the distinction of being selected as the league's Most Valuable Player. He was still in Rochester the next year when he played twenty-five games and then was inducted in the United States Army.

Up until the Army called him, Red's left eye had given him little trouble. But now, while he was playing baseball with an Army team, the eye again became inflamed and sore. After his discharge from the Army in 1945, Red visited an optometrist in St. Louis who prescribed exercises for the eye. Before long the eye felt better again.

In 1945, on the strength of his showing in minor-league ball, Red Schoendienst was called up to the St. Louis Cardinals. There was no room for the twenty-two-year-old redheaded kid in the Cardinal infield, which was already ably manned by Ray Sanders at first base, Emil Verban at second, Marty Marion at shortstop and Whitey Kurowski at third. But Cardinal manager Billy Southworth was impressed with Red's ability to hit well from either side of the plate, his speed on the bases, his fielding talents and his strong throwing arm, and he wanted to get Red into the starting lineup. Finally he decided to install young Schoendienst in left field.

Although he had played the infield all through his minor-league apprenticeship, Schoendienst took to the outfield like a duck to water. That year he batted .278 and exhibited speed by stealing 26 bases.

Eddie Dyer became the manager of the St. Louis Cardinals in 1946, and he felt that Schoendienst would make a better infielder than outfielder. He tried Red at every infield position but first base and finally decided to station him at second.

It was a good move because Schoendienst was an immediate success at his new spot. He was fast on his feet, with an ability to go to his right or left with equal grace and effectiveness. He had sure hands and could handle almost anything hit to him, and his speed, agility and footwork made him a key man on double plays.

Red had a highly successful 1946 season, hitting .281 and establishing himself as a steady infielder. But in 1947 his batting average slipped to .253 and there was some worry in the Cardinal front office about Schoendienst's work with the bat.

"You swing at too many bad pitches," manager Eddie Dyer told him. "You're too anxious up there. You're willing to take a cut at anything the pitcher throws you, instead of waiting for the pitch *you* want."

Schoendienst found it difficult to break the habit. In 1948 his batting average climbed to .272, but Dyer wasn't satisfied. The manager told him again that he was too anxious and that if he stopped swinging at every pitch he could become a .300 hitter.

In 1949 Red Schoendienst made a solid effort to discipline himself at the plate. It is said that every hitter gets an average of one good pitch to hit every time at bat, and Red waited for that pitch. His batting average rose to .297—the highest he had ever batted since joining the Cardinals—and Dyer said happily, "You're on your way."

Despite his hitting troubles, Schoendienst was by this time recognized as one of the finest second basemen in the National League. In 1949, for example, he set a record for second basemen by executing 320 consecutive plays without an error.

In 1950 Red's batting average slid back to .276, but this was the year he became a national hero in the All Star Game. He had appeared with the All Star squad in 1946, 1948 and 1949 but had not figured in many dramatics. Nor did it look as if he would in 1950, for he started the game sitting on the National League bench. Jackie Robinson, the great infielder for the Brooklyn Dodgers, held down the second-base position, and there seemed little chance that Schoendienst would see much action, if he played at all.

It was a close game all the way, and when nine innings were completed the score was National League 3, American League 3. The game went into the tenth inning, the first time in the seventeen-game All Star series that a contest had gone into extra innings.

The tenth inning passed without either team's scoring, and in the top of the eleventh the National League mounted a bases-loaded threat but failed to score. As the American Leaguers prepared to take their bats in the bottom of the eleventh, the National League manager, Burt Shotton, turned to Schoendienst on the bench.

"Go out and play second," he said.

Red grabbed his glove and trotted out to relieve Jackie Robinson at second.

The game remained scoreless in the eleventh, twelfth and thirteenth innings. In the top of the fourteenth Red Schoendienst was the lead-off batter, the first time he had batted in the game.

The 46,000 fans in the stands were strangely quiet. They knew this was probably the most exciting All Star game yet played, and they knew it could be broken up by one big break—a home run, an error, a wild pitch, almost anything. And they were waiting.

Red Schoendienst took his position in the batter's box, choking the bat high. He had never been a long-ball hitter, and all he wanted to do was punch out a base hit and let the big guns drive him around.

Ted Gray, a Detroit left-hander, was pitching for the AL and he studied Schoendienst, noted how he choked the bat and decided he had little to fear from Jackie Robinson's substitute. Gray toed the rubber, went into his stretch, brought his arms down, hesitated momentarily, then fired the pitch. Schoendienst swung.

What happened was totally unexpected. No one in the ball park—least of all Schoendienst—expected it to happen. But the ball Schoendienst hit went on a line to left field, climbed as it traveled, and sailed over outfielder Dominic DiMaggio's head into the left-field seats for a home run!

It was an unforgettable All Star moment, and, since the American League failed to score in the bottom of the fourteenth, Red's homer won the ballgame!

The game has gone down in baseball history as one of the more memorable All Star contests.

Despite this momentary display of power, Schoendienst remained primarily a singles hitter and did not hit the .300 mark in batting until 1952, when he finished with an average of .303. Then, in 1953, he hit .342, only two points less than Carl Furillo of the Brooklyn Dodgers, who won the batting title with .344. In 1954 Red stayed in the .300 class with .315, but the next year his injured eye began to trouble him again and his batting average tumbled to .268.

The 1956 season did not look promising for Red Schoendienst. Although exercising his eye muscles during the off-season had helped his eye somewhat, his faulty sight still threatened his career as a major-leaguer. His age was also a growing factor. He was now thirty-three years old and, in addition to the eye problem, an old injury to his right shoulder became inflamed. For a while he could hardly throw the ball.

In the St. Louis front office, general manager Frank Lane, a compulsive trader, figured Schoendienst's best days were behind him and decided to peddle him while other clubs still thought he had some value. On June 14, 1956, Schoendienst —one of the most popular second sackers in Cardinal history—was dealt off to the New York Giants in a wild eight-player trade that brought Whitey Lockman, Don Liddle and Alvin Dark to the Cardinals.

Schoendienst hated to leave St. Louis. He was popular with both the fans and his teammates, and his long-time roommate, Stan Musial, was the best friend he had. Besides, he did not agree with Frank Lane that he was washed up. He felt strongly that he had years of good baseball still in him.

Angered and disappointed, Red sat on the New York bench for two weeks until his shoulder improved, then went out and played 92 games for the Giants, batting .302 for the season. Not only that, he made only two errors all season long. The season brought Red a measure of satisfaction, for he had proved by his performance that he could still play major-league ball.

Despite his good year, the Giants traded Schoendienst off one year after they got him. On June 15, 1957, the Giants sent Red to the Milwaukee Braves in exchange for three solid major-league players—Bobby Thomson, Danny O'Connell and Ray Crone.

Baseball experts considered the trade a lopsided one in favor of the Giants. But the Milwaukee Braves knew what they were doing. There was no one on their club capable of on-the-field leadership, and they were certain Schoendienst was the inspirational player they needed to fill that role.

They were right. Schoendienst inspired the entire club by batting .309, hitting 15 home runs and, along with short-stop Johnny Logan, giving the Braves one of the best double-play combinations in the National League. Milwaukee won the pennant and went on to defeat the highly favored New York Yankees in the 1957 World Series, four games to three.

Red Schoendienst's play in 1957 was the main reason why the experts picked the Braves to repeat in 1958. But what they did not know was that a series of injuries and illnesses was to reduce Red's value to the team that year.

In spring training and for the first couple weeks of the regular season, Schoendienst suffered from a groin injury that dated back to the previous season. In May, just after recovering from the groin problem, he hurt his side sliding into a base. During the summer months he had an attack of pleurisy and then broke a finger on his left hand. He played only intermittently during the summer, but in August he forced himself back into the lineup because another infielder was hurt.

He played in pain the rest of the season. Pains in his chest caused by the pleurisy were acute, and often it was an effort for him even to breathe. As a result of all his miseries, Schoendienst's batting average tumbled to .262, his second lowest average in seventeen years of organized ball.

Still, the Braves won the pennant again in 1958 and battled the same New York Yankees in the World Series. This time the Yanks won, four games to three, despite the fact that Schoendienst overcame his miseries when the chips were down and turned in a stellar job. He embarrassed the opposition with nine hits, including three doubles and a triple, and fielded with great skill—but when he went home after the season, the chest pains were worse and he was coughing violently.

It was then that Schoendienst decided to have a thorough physical examination. Among other things the doctor took an X-ray of his lungs; when he looked at the plate and noticed a shadow on Red's right lung, he turned to Schoendienst and said:

"I hope this plate is lying, but I don't think it is."

Schoendienst was placed in the hospital and examined by two other physicians. All of the doctors concurred in the prognosis: the stellar second baseman was the victim of tuberculosis. He was immediately transferred to Mount St. Rose Hospital, which specialized in TB cases, and doctors said that Schoendienst would not be leaving the hospital until spring at the earliest.

The big question, of course, had to do with Schoendienst's future. Would Red ever play baseball again? The doctors wouldn't say. Red was close to thirty-six years old now, and it would be impossible for him to recover in time for the start of the 1959 season. It was likely that he would miss the entire year. Could he, then, at age thirty-seven, hope to make a comeback after a bout with TB?

No one really thought he could, but the Milwaukee Braves signed him to a 1959 contract anyway, making the gesture in his honor.

In the clinically white room of Mount St. Rose Sanitarium, Red Schoendienst bid good-bye to his wife, Mary, and their two children, and found himself virtually isolated from the world he knew. His life in the hospital was strictly regimented—a shower in the morning, the rest of the day in bed, pills five times a day to arrest the infection. His only entertainment was reading newspapers, and letters from friends and fans, and watching television.

By February the antibiotics Red was taking had contained the tuberculosis, reducing the infection to the upper lobe of his right lung. Surgeons then cut away the diseased portion of the lung.

Meanwhile, spring training had started and Red's Milwaukee teammates had gone south. Schoendienst fretted at his inaction, but there was nothing he could do about it. Finally, on March 24, he was released from the hospital.

Returning home greatly encouraged, Red had dreams of playing baseball again in a short time. But he soon found that the recovery period was to be a lengthy one and there would be no opportunity to return to baseball for the 1959 season. By midsummer, however, he was able to play catch at his home as his weakness left him. Each day he felt a little stronger; each day his hopes were raised a notch or two.

Actually, toward the end of the 1959 major-league season, Red made a few token appearances with the Braves. He played briefly in five games, went to the plate three times but had no hits. The Milwaukee Braves finished second that year, and how much of their failure to win the pennant again was traceable to Schoendienst's absence will never be known. But there is no doubt that the team missed him.

By spring, 1960, Schoendienst had fully recovered from his ordeal and was back at his accustomed place at second base when the season opened. He was now thirty-seven, and the question that swept the National League changed. It was no longer "Would he ever play baseball again?" It was "Can Schoendienst make a comeback from such a severe illness and pick up his career at the age of thirty-seven?"

Red Schoendienst answered this question by his play on the field. In the Braves' 1960 opener against the Pittsburgh Pirates, Red was the pivot man on two fast double plays, and there seemed to be no letup in the speed with which he performed these duties. The next day he stroked two hits and two days later added four more. TB patient Red Schoendienst was away and running.

What he accomplished in 1960 is a tribute to Red Schoendienst's talents and his courage. Although he played in only 68 games—with manager Charlie Dressen resting him frequently—he batted .257 and fielded his position with his usual skill. This was a good season for a man who had come back from a hospital bed, but apparently the Milwaukee Braves decided it was not good enough. Believing that Red was at the end of his career, the Braves gave him his unconditional release at the end of the season.

Red was shocked at the sudden turn of events, but as it developed the move was a favorable one for Red. The St.

Louis Cardinals, for whom he had played eleven years, picked him up again, and he was reunited with his best friend, Stan Musial. He served as a player-coach on the Cardinals in 1961, 1962 and half of 1963. In 1961 he played in 72 games and batted an even .300; in 1962 he played 98 games and hit .301. His active playing days ended on July 9, 1963, and he was appointed a full-time coach.

Then, on October 20, 1964, Red Schoendienst was named manager of the St. Louis Cardinals, completing a career that was one of the most distinguished in baseball history. Red Schoendienst had overcome an eye injury in his youth that diminished his sight, struggled through serious injuries during his major-league career and finally fought his way back from a bout with tuberculosis to finish a career that marked him as one of the finest players in the game. Finally, adding new luster to his shiny career, Red was named manager of the team he had served so long and so well.

Red Schoendienst was not the greatest second baseman in baseball or the greatest hitter, but no one can deny that he was one of the most courageous.

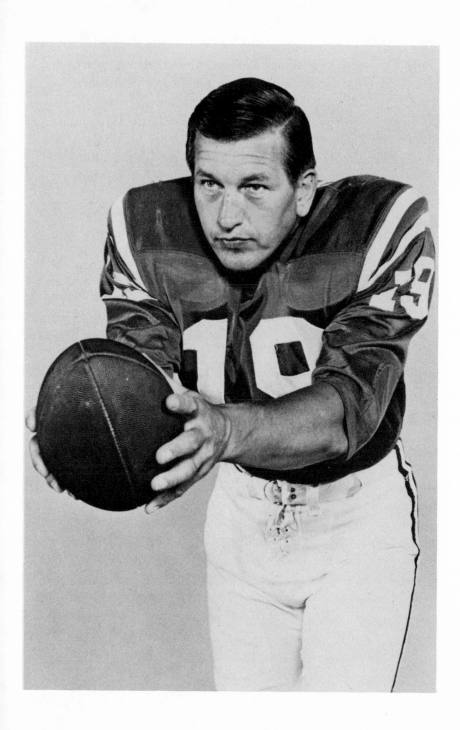

6

Johnny Unitas . . .
the football player nobody wanted

He was the football player nobody wanted. Colleges shunned him. So did the pros. Whenever his name came up, the verdict was always the same. He was too small.

His name was Johnny Unitas, and he was to become one of the greatest quarterbacks—some say *the* greatest—in professional football.

He was born John Constantine Unitas on May 7, 1933, in Pittsburgh, one of four Unitas children. His father, who drove a coal delivery truck, passed away when Johnny was five years old, leaving the burden of taking care of the family to Johnny's mother. His mother was a stalwart person, accustomed to hardship and not afraid of work. She managed to support the four Unitas children by keeping the coal business going for a while, working in a bakery and serving as a scrubwoman in public buildings. She even found time to sell insurance and study bookkeeping.

Young Johnny knew hard labor early in life. He had to help his older brother, Len, load the coal truck. His mother drove it. Existence was a family project.

By the time Johnny was old enough to enter St. Justin's High School in Pittsburgh, he had already developed some muscular hardness, although he weighed only 130 pounds. He had always been interested in football—in fact, dreamed when he was a boy of becoming a famous player—and one of the first things he did was join the high school team as a freshman. He made the team without trouble and played at halfback during his freshman and sophomore years.

His talent as a pass-throwing quarterback might have gone undiscovered had it not been for an injury to the team's regular quarterback during Johnny's junior year. Rushed into action as an emergency substitute, Johnny displayed the power and accuracy of his throwing arm. He won the job as quarterback, and in his last two years at St. Justin's he threw twenty-two touchdown passes and was named to the Pittsburgh All-Catholic team in both years.

High school football whetted Johnny Unitas' appetite for the game, and he decided he simply had to play at one of the nation's top colleges. His mother was not financially able to send Johnny to college, which meant he would have to try for an athletic scholarship. He prevailed upon one of his high school teachers, the Reverend Thomas J. McCarthy, to contact Notre Dame. If he could play with a college like Notre Dame, he thought, he would get the visibility he needed to move on to the pros after his graduation.

By this time Johnny had sprouted to six feet, but he still weighed only 145 pounds. Nevertheless, he had a one-week tryout at Notre Dame—an act that got him no place. The verdict on his performance shocked him. Notre Dame coaches regretfully told him that he would never be big enough to play college football.

Johnny was fated to hear that verdict many times. He was turned down by Indiana University, the University of Maryland and Lehigh University, and always for the same reason: he was too small.

It was nearing the time for the fall semester to begin, and Johnny's chances of catching on with a college team seemed hopeless. One day he heard that a tryout for football was being held at the University of Louisville. At first he was inclined to ignore it. Louisville was a small college with a weak national reputation, and Johnny was afraid he could gain no recognition there even if he made the team. But time was slipping away, and finally he presented himself to Coach Frank Camp. He ran, he threw and he tackled, and when it was all over, Camp looked him up and down and Johnny imagined he heard the words again: *too small*. But instead Camp said, "I think you might put on a few pounds yet, and you *can* throw the ball. You've got a free ride."

The University of Louisville offered Johnny Unitas an athletic scholarship, and Johnny was both happy and sad about it. It was not the kind of school he wanted to play for, but at least he would be able to play.

Since Louisville was not a member of the National Collegiate Athletic Association, freshmen were eligible to play on the varsity. Johnny made the team—as a bench-warming third-string quarterback.

Louisville did not have much of a football team. They were perennial losers. And in 1951 the team started out in the usual fashion, losing its first four games. Then came a game with St. Bonaventure.

This game started out like all the others. St. Bonaventure rolled up a 19-0 lead in the first half, and in the dressing room Frank Camp decided he had to do something drastic. His eyes traveled over the team and settled on the lanky, 145-pound Unitas.

"You start the second half at quarterback," he told Johnny.

A wave of excitement swept over Unitas, and he pranced out on the field for the second half like a young colt. He promptly gave St. Bonaventure the scare of its life. Leading the team with skill and imagination, he completed eleven passes in a row, three of them for touchdowns, and guided Louisville to a 21-19 lead. A stunned St. Bonaventure team finally managed to kick a field goal in the dying minutes to salvage a 22-21 victory, but it was a big day for Johnny Unitas.

His startling performance earned him the job of first-string quarterback.

What happened after that was extremely exciting for Coach Frank Camp and his Louisville team. Young Unitas led Louisville to victories in the last four games of the season, tossing eight TD passes in the process. He had turned the lowly Louisville team around with his leadership and passing skills.

It would be nice to say that Unitas led the Louisville team to winning records in his next three years, but the team was so mediocre that this was impossible. Nevertheless, he managed to salvage a few unexpected victories for Louisville, and in the process he built himself a reputation. By the time he had finished his senior year, he had completed 245 passes in 502 attempts, chalked up 2,912 yards and hit on 27 touchdown passes.

He had also put on some weight, tipping the scales at 195 pounds and standing six-feet-one.

Word of Johnny Unitas' four years at Louisville had reached

the front office of the professional Pittsburgh Steelers, and when the National Football League draft of college players took place, the Steelers chose Unitas as their eighth draft choice. Johnny was beside himself with joy. Here was an opportunity to play professional football—the thing he had always wanted—and to play it right in his own home town!

It was July, 1955, and Unitas was practically the first man to report to the Steeler training camp in Olean, New York. To his chagrin, he found there were three quarterbacks on the roster, each with more experience than he had. Walt Kiesling, the Pittsburgh coach, watched Unitas' performance with interest and noted that he threw the ball with accuracy, but he just did not have room for him. When the Steelers broke camp, he took Johnny aside.

"I'm sorry," he said, "but we have to release you."

He handed Unitas a ten-dollar bill as transportation expense back to his home in Pittsburgh.

The blow was a tough one to take. Suddenly, all his dreams had collapsed around him. It was a time when a lesser man might have folded up and decided professional football just wasn't for him. But Unitas did not give up. When he got home, he sent a telegram to Coach Paul Brown of the Cleveland Browns. Johnny had heard that the Browns were having trouble finding a good quarterback. Otto Graham, who had held the position for years, had decided to retire from football, and the position was wide open for anybody who could qualify.

What Johnny did not know was that Otto Graham had been talked into postponing his retirement for a year. Paul Brown wired Unitas back, saying that he had no need for a new quarterback this season and suggesting that Unitas contact him again the following year.

The year that followed was one of the toughest of Johnny's life. He took a job as a piledriver with a construction gang— hard, back-breaking work that would at least keep him in condition. In addition, he joined a semi-pro team called the Bloomfield Rams, because he did not want to lose his "touch" as a football player. He was paid six dollars a game by the Rams, and he played football on unkempt fields covered with dangerous ruts and rocks. But it helped him to keep in physical shape, and it gave him an opportunity to improve his passing.

Johnny continued to work with the construction gang after the Rams' season ended, and in February he received an unexpected phone call. It was from Don Kellett, the general manager of the Baltimore Colts.

"We're looking for a number-two quarterback to replace Gary Kerkorian," Kellett said. "If you're interested, why not come down to our tryout camp in May? Coach Weeb Ewbank will look you over, and if you have the stuff you'll be invited to our regular summer training camp with a chance to make the team."

Johnny forgot all about the mild interest the Browns had shown in him and accepted the Colts' offer almost before Kellett had finished telling him about it. He showed up at the May training camp and threw the football around in a manner that opened Weeb Ewbank's eyes. His efforts earned him an invitation to the regular training camp, where he opened the coach's eyes again. Johnny Unitas made the team as the second-string quarterback behind the regular, George Shaw, at a salary of $7,000.

At last, Johnny Unitas thought, *I've landed with a professional football club. At last the dream has been realized. Now, if I can only get into a game.*

The opportunity came sooner than Unitas expected. The Colts were playing the Bears at Chicago when Shaw broke his leg in a pile-up. Ewbank, on the sideline, crooked a finger at Unitas, huddled on the bench.

"Here's your chance, John," he said. "Go in there and just do your best."

Unitas raced on the field, adjusting the strap on his helmet as he went. He called the play in the huddle, then crouched behind the center and barked out the signals. He felt the ball snap into his hands and faded back to pass. He spotted a receiver downfield and let the ball go. But it all went wrong. The pass was intercepted by the Chicago Bears' J. C. Caroline, who ran it back for a touchdown.

Johnny's face went red with embarrassment. One play, one pass—and disaster!

From that time on, everything fell apart for Unitas. Three times he fumbled a handoff, and three times the Bears recovered and went on to touchdowns. When the carnage was over, Chicago had beaten the Baltimore Colts, 58-27.

It was a terrible debut, and Unitas felt sick about it. But Coach Ewbank didn't hold the poor performance against him. "He came off the bench ice cold," he said, and explained that he hadn't really had a chance to work with the first-string backfield. "I think he'll help us," he added.

Unitas appreciated the vote of confidence, even though he was aware that Ewbank had no choice but to use him, with Shaw out for an indefinite period. Johnny Unitas would be the starting quarterback against the Green Bay Packers the following weekend. And he was determined to make up for his calamitous first game.

Unitas did just that. He was on target with his passes against Green Bay, completing eight out of sixteen, two of them for touchdowns, and defeating the Packers, 28-21. The next week the Baltimore Colts beat the Cleveland Browns, 21-7, and much of the credit went to Unitas for his passing and play calling. Then the Colts dropped one against the Detroit Lions, 27-3, although Unitas passed for a stunning 324 yards.

But nothing Unitas did that season equaled his game against the Los Angeles Rams. He treated the Colts' fans at Baltimore's Memorial Stadium to the biggest football game ever played there when he completed 18 out of 24 passes for a total yardage of 293 and three touchdowns as the Colts romped over Los Angeles by a lopsided 56-21 score.

The Colts dropped three games after that, but in their final game against the Washington Redskins they won in the last fifteen seconds on a 53-yard pass by Unitas. The score was 19-17.

The following year, Unitas took up where he had left off in 1956. Going into the last two games, the Colts had won seven games and lost three and were in a hot race for the Western Division Championship. But they lost their last two games, finishing with 7-5—the first time in its history that Baltimore had finished above .500.

In 1958 Baltimore fielded a good running team and, along with Unitas' shrewd play calling and daring passes, they were definitely championship material. And they proved it immediately by winning their first six games. When the season ended, they had won nine and lost only one, grabbing the Western Division title. The New York Giants had won their division in the East, which meant that Baltimore and New York would face each other for the National Football League championship.

The game between the Baltimore Colts and the New York

Giants for the NFL championship has been called "the great-est football game ever played." It probably deserves the des-ignation, for it was certainly the most dramatic. It was played on a bitter cold day at venerable Yankee Stadium, with nearly 65,000 fans huddled in overcoats and underneath blankets. Those fans saw a game that made football history.

It was a game that pitted the tough offensive play of the Baltimore Colts against the stubborn defense of the New York Giants. New York fans were sure the Giants would stop Balti-more cold and win the game, probably by a small margin. The Baltimore fans were just as sure that the Colts' runners and the fine passing of Unitas would bury the Giants.

The Giants got on the board first. They worked the ball into Colts' territory in the first period, but their drive stalled. Pat Summerall then dropped back and booted a thirty-six-yard field goal to put the Giants ahead, 3-0. But the Colts roared back in the second period to score two touchdowns, one on a pass from Unitas to Raymond Berry, and they trotted into the dressing room at half-time with a 14-3 lead.

But in the second half the Giants showed they were not a team to be trifled with. They stopped every drive the Colts started, took away the ball and began moving. They scored one touchdown to close the gap to 14-10, then scored another to take the lead, 17-14.

The clock ticked away the time. The Giants played a ball-control game, eating up time. The desperate Colts, seeing their dreams of the championship going up in smoke, didn't get their hands on the ball until the clock showed only two min-utes to play!

They were on their own 14-yard line, 86 long yards from the Giants' goal line. They didn't even have a time-out left to stop the clock and save precious seconds between plays.

Their problem was to move the ball close enough to try a field goal and force a tie. And since the NFL championship game could not end in a tie, the two teams would then be forced to battle each other in "sudden-death" overtime, and the first one to score would then be the winner.

But first they had to get the tie, and there wasn't very much time to do it in.

Johnny Unitas rushed into the huddle. "We haven't any time for huddles," he snapped. "I'll call the plays at the scrimmage line. Now we're going to find out which is the best team."

Johnny Unitas started to throw passes. He threw seven of them in a row—to Raymond Berry for 25 yards, to Lenny Moore for 11, to Berry again for 15, over and over—and suddenly the Colts found themselves on the Giants' 13-yard line with only seconds to go.

Unitas might have won the game right there with one more pass, but there was no time. They had to go for the tie, and Steve Myrha, the Colts' field-goal kicker, ran onto the field. Standing on the 20, he kicked the ball through the uprights, and the game was tied 17-17 just as the gun sounded!

Johnny Unitas, ice cold and devastated, had driven his team from its own 14-yard line to the Giants' 13 with the pinpoint accuracy of his passes, and for the first time in NFL history the contending teams would go into a 15-minute overtime period.

This was nerve-racking football. Now neither team could allow the other to get close enough even for a try at a field goal, for any score of any kind would end the game. And, to make matters worse, from the Colts' viewpoint, they were required to kick off to the Giants.

The whistle blew, and the kick arched through the air to

settle down near the Giants' goal line. The Colts raced after it and downed the runner inside the 20. Three plays by the Giants failed, and the Giants were forced to punt.

The Colts' defensive unit had done its job. Now the Colts would get the ball, and it would be up to Johnny Unitas and Company to win the game.

The Colts received the ball on their own 20 and started play from that point. Eighty yards away was the beckoning goal line of the Giants. Eighty long yards that had to be covered, somehow, with cleverly mixed passes and running plays—and it was up to Johnny Unitas to find the way.

Unitas opened the drive with a running play, handing off to L. G. Dupre, who turned the right end for ten yards and a quick first down at the 30. On the next play Unitas tried a pass, but it fell incomplete. Dupre tried the middle of the line and picked up only three. Third down and seven coming up— an important play.

Unitas faded back to pass and hit fullback Alan Ameche, a galloping horse of a man, who galloped to the Colts' 40-yard line—just enough to make the first down.

Again Unitas faded back to pass. Huge Giant defenders came in on him and dumped him for a 12-yard loss. Second down and 22 yards to go. It looked as if the Giants had stopped the Colts in their tracks.

But Unitas went back again to pass. Again the red-dogging linebackers closed in on him. He scrambled to the right, to the left, to avoid the tacklers. But suddenly he spotted Raymond Berry all the way down on the Giants' 42-yard line. He let the pass go, and it carried like a bullet into Berry's arms. First down in Giant territory!

Would they get close enough for a field goal that would win the game? The Giant fans in the stands were on the edge of their seats. A great fear swept over them. Unitas was the picture of determination out there, and the Giants appeared to be caving in under his onslaught.

Ameche rammed up the middle of the line, and suddenly the Colts were on the Giants' 23-yard line with a first down. They were close enough to kick a field goal that would end the game.

But Unitas wanted to get closer. He gave the ball to Dupre, and the Giants stopped him for no gain. Again Unitas faded back, and again the Giants rushed him; but he got the ball away to Berry, and it was first down on the Giants' eight!

The Giant fans looked at the Colts' bench, expecting to see Steve Myrha, the field-goal kicker, come in. But he didn't, and their eyes returned to the field. What would Unitas try now?

Unitas handed off again, and Ameche tried the center of the Giant line. The Giants stopped him with only a one-yard gain. The Giants figured there would be a couple more such plays, running plays that would keep the ball on the ground, and then there would be a field-goal try on fourth down.

But Unitas rarely did what the other team was expecting. Instead, with second down on the seven, he took to the air again—a pass in the right flat that was extremely dangerous. But the unexpectedness of the play made it a success. Jim Mutscheller grabbed it and was tackled on the Giants' one-yard line!

Third down, one yard to go. One yard away from victory in this NFL championship game, this most dramatic game in professional football history!

Unitas handed the ball to the bull-like Ameche. He hit the right side of the Giants' line. The Giants tried desperately to stop the charge, but Ameche smashed his way over the goal line for the touchdown.

The game ended abruptly. Colts 23, Giants 17!

As long as football is played, this game will be remembered as "the greatest."

From that time on, it was uphill all the way for Unitas. His pinpoint passing and great play-calling ability quickly established him as one of the great quarterbacks of NFL history. He did everything a quarterback is expected to do, and more. In one unbelievable string of 47 games he threw a touchdown pass in each one. He has thrown more passes, has completed more and has more touchdown passes to his credit than any other player in professional football history, and each time he walks out on the field he adds to his totals.

There is no doubt he belongs with the great quarterbacks of history—Bobby Layne, Sid Luckman, Otto Graham, Slingin' Sammy Baugh and Y. A. Tittle. In fact, the "football player nobody wanted" will probably go down in football history as the greatest of all time.

7

Doak Walker . . .
the midget who played with giants

He did not look like a football player. Not when he ran out onto the field with the rest of the Detroit Lions, anyway. He stood five-feet-eleven and weighed 170 pounds; alongside the 200- and 250-pound behemoths who thundered over the grassy turf as the Lions prepared to meet the Pittsburgh Steelers, he looked like a midget among men.

A fan in the stands, particularly knowledgeable about professional football, said to his companion, "The Steelers will pick that guy up and toss him off the field. How can a little guy like that take the pounding these pros dish out?"

"He had a great college career," said the other man.

"So what's a college career?" snorted the first man. "In college you can weigh 170 pounds and get away with it. But in the pros? Forget it, man!" He shook his head sadly. "I don't think I shoulda come. I hate the sight of blood."

The two fans were talking about a young man who, fresh out of Southern Methodist University, had joined the Lions for the 1950 season. The Lions had opened their season away from home, defeating Green Bay, and this young man had contributed two field goals. That wasn't much. As a halfback,

83

he would be required to run with the ball, and most of the fans thought that if he tried it the slaughter would be frightful. His name was Doak Walker.

Ewell Doak Walker, Jr., was born on January 2, 1924, in Dallas, Texas. His father, Ewell Doak Walker, Sr., was a school teacher in the Dallas public schools and had played football during his college days. Still an avid football follower, the elder Walker decided early that he would make a football player out of his son. By the time the youngster was six years old, he had learned to throw and kick a football with unusual skill. Only one thing disappointed his father. Young Doak was not growing very fast, and the elder Walker began to realize that Doak would never be as big a man as he had hoped.

When Doak (he preferred to be called by his middle name) entered Highland Park High School in Dallas, it was doubtful if his size would permit him to play football. But he went out for the team and made it on the strength of his ball-handling skills, and in 1943 and 1944 he became a star performer whose name spread throughout the state of Texas. With him on the team was another young man who was destined to make it big in professional football—a kid named Bobby Layne.

Before Doak finished high school, he earned letters in football, baseball, basketball, track and swimming. World War II was still raging when Doak graduated, and he immediately joined the United States Maritime Service. Within ten months the war ended and he was released. Doak then enrolled at Southern Methodist University (SMU).

Southern Methodist was halfway through a troublesome season when Doak arrived on the scene. Freshmen were allowed to play on the varsity squad in those days, and five days after joining the team Doak found himself playing at halfback against SMU's traditional rival, the University of Texas Longhorns. The Longhorns were expected to whip the SMU Mustangs handily.

It would be nice to report that Doak turned the game around by defeating Texas, but he didn't do quite that. He did inspire SMU to put up a fierce battle against the Longhorns, and in the first half he threaded his way 29 yards through the Texas team for Southern Methodist's only touchdown. But his old high school buddy, Bobby Layne, happened to be pitching passes for Texas that afternoon, and he connected on two of them to make the final score Texas 12, SMU 7.

However, Doak's performance was so outstanding that the *Dallas Morning News* reported his activities this way:

"In five days Doak Walker transformed the SMU Mustangs from Southwest Conference cellar candidates into a serious aspirant for the championship; from an inconsistent, lethargic, mistake-smitten organization into a fiery, determined and efficient machine. He passed, he ran, he caught passes, punted on occasion, and played a terrific game."

Primarily as a result of Doak's play, the SMU Mustangs finished second to Texas in the Southwest Conference. Walker was named on the All-Southwest Conference team and played for the West in the East-West game on New Year's Day. The game ended in a 7-7 tie, but it was Walker's play in the last quarter that brought the West back from a 7-0 deficit to tie the game.

Walker joined the Army and spent the 1946 season in uniform. But he returned the following year and led Southern Methodist to one of its finest seasons.

There was no stopping Walker or the SMU team. They won

five straight games—against Santa Clara, Missouri, Oklahoma A&M, UCLA and Rice—and Doak was the key figure in most of them. Against Santa Clara, he returned a kickoff 96 yards, romped 44 yards for another TD and led the team on a 56-yard march for a third touchdown. In a wild lopsided victory over Missouri, he had a 76-yard punt return and a 57-yard touchdown run to ice the game.

With five games on the winning side of the ledger, SMU found itself facing the formidable Texas Longhorns again. Texas had won six games in a row, and had such a powerful team that most fans thought they were a shoo-in to beat SMU. They had not counted on the remarkable Doak. In a grim battle that saw Texas holding a 13-7 lead that threatened to endure, Doak Walker finally took the ball on SMU's own 43-yard line, turned the corner at end and galloped 57 yards for a touchdown to tie the score. He then calmly kicked the extra point to give SMU a 14-13 victory.

Southern Methodist went on, then, to win three more games, taking an undefeated record into its last game with Texas Christian. Then came trouble. Texas Christian battled valiantly and had a 19-13 lead with only twenty seconds of play remaining. It looked hopeless to everyone but Doak. Walker led his team in a fight against the clock, and the Mustangs tied the score, 19-19, with only seconds remaining.

SMU's record of ten wins and one tie earned them a trip to the Cotton Bowl, where they played a rugged Penn State outfit to a 13-13 tie. Walker passed for one of SMU's touchdowns and ran for the other. The Doaker, as he had come to be known, was awarded the Maxwell Trophy as the nation's outstanding college player.

The following year Doak repeated his performance, leading Southern Methodist to another Conference championship and getting them into the Cotton Bowl again. This time they defeated the University of Oregon, 21-13, with Doak completing six out of ten passes.

The 1949 season was disastrous for both Doak Walker and SMU. The graduation of most of its best players left the team without muscle. Shortly after the season opened, Walker was hurt and missed most of the games. But he had already made an impression on the professional football scouts. As soon as he graduated, he was deluged with offers. Big bonuses were not paid in those days—nor were big salaries—and the best offer was a three-year contract at $15,000 a year from the Detroit Lions. They wanted the flashy college player to put some spark in a team that had suffered four bad seasons in a row and looked as if it was content to go on that way.

Doak made the team, and when the Lions opened their season against Green Bay, he helped the team score a 45-7 win by kicking two field goals—not a performance that made much of an impression on Detroit's disgruntled fans. The next Sunday the Lions met the Pittsburgh Steelers, and Walker was slated to start at halfback.

Detroit fans were in a show-me attitude. They were not at all sure of this guy they called the Doaker. To them, he hardly looked like a remarkable addition to the Lions' team. He was probably just another college kid who would play a few games as a pro, find the going too rough and fade out of the league. There were many like him.

It was September 24, 1950, a date that lives in the minds of Lions fans. The game was played under gray skies that threatened a rain that never came. It turned out to be a bruising defensive battle, with each team yielding yards grudgingly. When the first half was over, the scoreboard showed two goose eggs—0-0.

Until this time Doak Walker had played a creditable game but had done nothing spectacular. When the second half opened, the Lions had to kick off to the Steelers, who carried the ball back to their own 28. From that point they began to move—slowly, methodically, like some great machine, grinding out yardage, bit by bit, until they covered the 72 yards necessary for the touchdown. The extra point sailed between the uprights, and the score was Steelers 7, Lions 0.

Doak Walker was one of those players who thrive best in adversity. When his team fell behind in the score, it did something to the little man from Texas. His adrenalin flowed, his spirit rose and he began to do the things he was capable of doing—running, side-stepping, catching passes, kicking. Still, despite his efforts, the Steelers held off the Lions during the third period.

But now the Lions were in a good scoring position. The third period had ended with the Lions owning a first down on the Steelers' 11-yard line.

The Doaker ran his pass pattern, to the left and then cutting sharply toward the end zone; when he looked around, the ball was in the air, spiraling toward him. A Pittsburgh defender was right on him, and the two went into the air for the ball. Doak caught it on his fingertips, gathered it in and fell in the end zone for a touchdown. Walker then kicked the extra point to tie the score, 7-7.

In the final quarter both teams slugged it out, but again the defense dominated the play on both sides. With three minutes to go in the game, the score was still deadlocked, 7-7, and the Lions had the ball deep in their own territory.

It was fourth down, and Walker dropped back to punt. His kick was high and had distance, coming down into the waiting arms of Bobby Gage, the Steelers' safety man, on the 15-yard

line. Just as he caught it, he was hit with a thudding tackle—
and fumbled. A Lion player fell on the ball and, suddenly,
Detroit had the football on the Steelers' 15-yard stripe.

It was the kind of break that often decides close defensive
battles. The clock was ticking away on the scoreboard. The
Lions tried three running plays and went nowhere. There was
only one thing to do—try for a field goal.

Doak Walker was the kicker, and he aimed the ball for the
uprights. It was a perfect kick from the 20-yard line, and the
score was 10-7 in favor of the Lions. That's the way it ended.

Little Doak Walker—who wasn't supposed to be playing
with such big bruising men—had scored all of the Lions'
points. But he had done more than that. He had done all the
punting, and he had gained 87 yards in 16 tries against a
stout and stubborn Pittsburgh line.

The Doaker had established himself as a solid professional
football player, even if he didn't weigh as much as most of the
men on the field.

That was the beginning of a fine football season for the
midget from SMU. Despite a nagging ankle injury he suffered
halfway through the season, Doak Walker scored eleven touchdowns, booted 38 extra points and kicked eight field goals, for
a total of 128 points. His performance was only ten points shy
of the league record set by Don Hutson, a great Green Bay end,
in 1942, and was good enough to lead the National Football
League in 1950.

Doak Walker's running ability was one of his greatest as-
sets. He had a knack of hopscotching through a broken field,
had great balance and was shifty enough to fool many
would-be tacklers. In a race down the sidelines, he had no
peer. He could turn on the speed, pull up sharply to let a
tackler sail past him, then turn it on again. He also possessed

an uncanny accuracy with his toe, scoring extra points with little difficulty and kicking field goals from any spot in the field within range of the crossbars.

All of these talents showed themselves again when the 1951 season started. Bobby Layne, who had played with Doak in high school and against him in college, was the Lions' quarterback when the season opened. Layne was an excellent passer, but Walker was not far behind. Opposing teams went out of their minds trying to figure out what offensive strategy the Lions might employ, because on one play Layne would pass to Walker and on the next Walker would pass to Layne.

With this combination, plus Pat Harder, a line plunger who could rip his own holes in the defensive line of any team, the Lions were definite threats in the championship race, and when the season ground down to the last game the Lions were in first place, hanging on by the skin of their teeth to a half-game lead over the Los Angeles Rams and Chicago Bears. In the wind-up game of the season, the Lions had to meet the San Francisco Forty-Niners on the West Coast.

When the game started on the coast, the Lions already knew what had happened to the Bears. They had lost to the St. Louis Cardinals, and the defeat had knocked them out of the race. The championship would now become the property of either the Lions or the Los Angeles Rams.

The Rams were meeting the Green Bay Packers in Los Angeles, and it soon became evident that the Rams were red hot. They built up a big lead on the Packers, and that put the pressure on the Lions to win if they were to grab the championship. They felt it too, because the Forty-Niners trotted off the field at half time with a 14-10 lead.

The Lions came back on the field for the third quarter determined to score. Bobby Layne began to click with his passes.

Pat Harder began to gain through the line. It was tough, rugged going, but they smashed their way 75 yards and crossed the Forty-Niners' goal line to make the score Lions 17, Forty-Niners 14.

They fought desperately, then, to hold off the San Franciscans, but they failed. In the fourth quarter the Forty-Niners scored again and the Lions were beaten.

Having come so close to winning the NFL title, the Lions made an even bigger bid the next year. Doak Walker, who wanted a championship so badly it hurt him, was injured early in the season and missed the last nine games. Nevertheless, the intrepid Bobby Layne led the team into the championship play-off game with the Cleveland Browns.

Walker, just recovered from his aches and pains, returned to the lineup for the championship contest. The Lions won the game, 17-7, and Doak contributed a twisting run of 67 yards for one of the touchdowns.

Doak Walker played football for six seasons, then retired to take a business offer in Dallas. By that time he had scored 534 points, third highest in National Football League history at the time. When he retired, Edward J. Anderson, the Lions' general manager, had his No. 37 retired. Almost apologetically, he said: "We never did this before, but it's a little different in the Doaker's case."

It was different, all right. In a game played by big and heavy men, the little 170-pounder everyone said was too light and too fragile to play professional football proved that ability even in a small man had to be recognized.

That's why he became known as Doak the Giant Killer.

8

Ken Venturi . . .
case of the unsinkable golfer

It's difficult for any athlete to come back after a serious injury or prolonged illness lays him low. But Ken Venturi, one of the most intrepid professional golfers, did it twice—a double comeback from illnesses that would have ended the career of a lesser man. In fact, golfing experts thought, on both occasions, that Venturi had no chance in the world to ever compete again in a major tournament. What they did not consider was that the dedication, grit and determination of the man made him virtually unsinkable.

Kenneth Venturi was born on May 15, 1931, in San Francisco, California, the only child of Fred and Ethyl Venturi. His father was a ship's chandler dealing in marine supplies and worked at the Embarcadero at the time. An avid golfer, he later became the manager of the pro shop at the city-owned Harding Park golf course.

Ken Venturi was introduced to golf early in his childhood. As soon as he was old enough, he caddied at Harding Park, and it wasn't long before his father was teaching him to play the game. He exhibited an immediate talent for golf, and after a few years a local automobile dealer named Ed Lowry took an interest in him and introduced him to Byron Nelson, the former pro champion. Lowry hired Venturi as a car salesman, and Nelson took him under his wing as a golf pupil. Venturi listened and learned as Nelson systematically turned him into an above-average golfer.

Venturi won his first amateur tournament at the age of seventeen, grabbing off the San Francisco City Championship. He enjoyed some additional success in national junior tournaments and, in 1951, won the California State Amateur Championship. In 1952, at age twenty-one, he participated in the America Cup matches at Seattle and won in both singles and foursome play. And in 1953 he was a member of the Walker Cup team that defeated the British in Massachusetts.

This rapid rise in the world of golf was interrupted by a two-year hitch in the Army. Army life put a temporary halt to Venturi's progress as a golfer, but when he returned he was considered good enough to be invited to play in the 1956 Masters Tournament at Augusta, Georgia.

Success was coming so fast and easily for Venturi that he entered the Masters with what might have been a touch of overconfidence. Keeping a cool head and playing like an automaton that could not make a mistake, Venturi entered the last day of play with a four-stroke lead over the field. But the pressure was too much for the twenty-five-year-old Venturi, and he shot an 80 and lost the tournament to Jack Burke by one stroke.

It was a bitter pill to swallow, but Venturi could do nothing but take it and strive on. He won a few more tournaments and in the fall of 1956 decided it was time to join the professional ranks. In his first year on the pro circuit Venturi played brilliant golf, winning six tournaments that netted him earnings of $50,000—a phenomenal first year for any golfer. Among those winning efforts were the St. Paul Open, which he won with a record-tying 266, and the Milwaukee Open, where he shot a 13-under-par 267.

Venturi's second year (1958) was another good one. He wrapped up the Thunderbird Invitational, Phoenix Open, Baton Rouge Open and Chicago Open. Again that year he entered the Masters in Augusta (open to both amateurs and pros). He was determined that this time he would win it, and he went out on the first day and shot a remarkable 68 to take the lead over the field. On the second day he had a par 72, but he was still in the lead when the sun went down. He lost the lead on the third day but stayed in contention, and on the fourth and last day he caught the great Arnie Palmer on the sixth hole and the two stayed neck and neck until the 475-yard 13th. Then it happened. Palmer, playing with great talent, hit the green on his second shot and dropped in a twisting 18-foot putt for an eagle three. It was a crushing blow, and Venturi never recovered from it. Palmer went on to take the Masters.

Still, the year was not all bad for Venturi. He was now one of the top money makers on the pro circuit, and although he won only two titles in 1959, he earned $30,000. In 1960 he won two tournaments again—losing the Masters once more when Palmer came from behind with two birdies on the last two holes to beat him by a single stroke. But his total earnings for the year mounted to $41,230.

It seemed, at that moment, that nothing could keep Ken Venturi from becoming one of the great golfers of his time.

But fate is fickle; just when Venturi was riding the crest of success, disaster loomed. He did not know it then, but he was not to win another tournament for *three years*. Suddenly plagued by a rash of physical ailments that ruined his game, he saw his earnings dwindle from $41,230 in 1960 to $3,848 in 1963.

It was a discouraging three-year period for Venturi, because he was aware that he would have done much better had it not been for his worsening health. One of his major troubles was a painful chest disorder. Doctors ruled out heart trouble and thought that the pain was caused by a muscle spasm or a pinched nerve. But they were unable to diagnose the trouble with accuracy. Venturi found it difficult to raise his right arm high enough to comb his hair, and to accommodate this condition he had to flatten and shorten his once-perfect swing. As a result, his game suffered.

With his nerves shattered by the cruel punishment he took by playing three years with pain, a boyhood stammer came back. He tried psychiatry and even hypnotism to get over the stammer, but he could not conquer the speech defect.

By 1964 he had hit rock bottom.

No one thought that Ken Venturi would ever again approach the top of his profession. It was believed that, even if he should recover from his physical ailments, he would never be able to regain the fine touch he had lost.

But Venturi would not lay his clubs aside and quit. He kept playing until, almost miraculously, his undiagnosed illnesses began to slip away. The chest pains eased, the pain left his arm, the stammer stopped. He won minor tournaments at Pensacola and Doral, Florida, and thought he was on the way back. But he failed to survive the cuts at four important tournaments, including the St. Petersburg Open and Los Angeles Open.

It was a sad blow because it lent credence to what his golfing friends were saying—that, even though his pain had dis-

appeared, he had lost his touch over the bad three years he
had suffered and he would never get it back.

Of course, Venturi did not agree with this appraisal. In
June he stubbornly entered the Thunderbird Classic at West-
chester Country Club in New York, and it was here that he
really began the first of his two comebacks. Venturi played
well enough in the Thunderbird to place third and pick up
$6,250 in prize money—the first big check he had won in
three years. His performance in the Thunderbird encouraged
him to enter the Buick Open at Detroit the following week.
Again he finished third, this time winning $7,629.

Venturi was elated. He was sure he was getting back the
long-lost touch—if, indeed, he had ever lost it—and he immediately signed for the United States Open, to be played at the
Congressional Country Club in Washington, D.C. This tournament turned out to be such a tough, relentless battle that it
was almost Venturi's undoing. But it also showed the spirit of
a true champ.

Washington, in summer, is hot and humid, and during the
U.S. Open the temperatures hovered in the high 90s. Venturi,
who had suffered heat prostration before and seemed unusu-
ally susceptible to high temperatures, shot a 72 and 70 in the
first two days. These were reasonably good scores, but they
left him trailing the leader, Tommy Jacobs, by six strokes
with 36 holes yet to play.

It was June 20, 1964, and the tournament was to end with
a marathon 36 holes in a single day. The temperature had
reached a sizzling 100 degrees. It would be a tough day under
a blazing sun, and Venturi hoped he had the stamina, after
several years of illness, to finish the tournament.

In the morning round Venturi posted an unbelievable five-
under-par 30 for the first nine. But on the back nine the im-

placable heat began to get to him. He staggered weakly on the
16th hole, and he was shaking so badly on the 17th green that
he could barely hold the putter. Trembling, he flubbed his tee
shot on the 18th, but he still managed to finish the morning
session with a remarkable 66, which put him just two strokes
behind Jacobs.

On the way to the clubhouse for a 45-minute break, Venturi's knees buckled. He was helped to the locker room and
examined by Dr. John Everett, who found him suffering from
dehydration. The obvious question was: Could Venturi survive another 18 holes in such blast-furnace heat?

"I'm only two strokes behind," said Venturi. "I just have
to go on."

Venturi fortified himself with iced tea and several salt tablets and reported for the final 18 holes. But this time he had
the foresight to bring Dr. Everett—who had been given special
permission to accompany him during play—along with him.
It was a shrewd move that was to play a major role in the
final outcome.

Venturi didn't wait long to get even with Jacobs. On the
second hole he carded a par 3 as Jacobs took a 5—and the two
of them were tied. From that time on the two leaders fought
a stubborn duel. Dr. Everett watched Venturi closely. All
through the 18-hole endurance test he fed him iced tea in
carefully rationed proportions, applied cold towels to his neck
and kept him on a steady diet of salt tablets.

On the ninth hole Venturi forged ahead, scoring a birdie 4
as Jacobs took a 6. That put Venturi two up with nine holes
to go! Could he hang onto his lead, now, or would the heat
destroy him?

The blazing sun proved a pitiless enemy. Jacobs endured it
stoically, but the more susceptible Venturi began to feel weak

and dizzy. On the 14th hole, reeling under the sun's ferocious attack, he told a tournament official, "Slap a two-stroke penalty on me for slow play if you like, but I'm going to slow down."

After that he walked ploddingly from hole to hole, as if only half-conscious—but no penalty was exacted. Little by little he could feel his strength waning, and the fear of heat prostration plagued his mind. The concerned doctor kept feeding him salt tablets—12 in all.

Fatigued, sick and on the brink of collapse, Venturi still managed to stay ahead of the healthier Jacobs. When the ordeal finally ended, he had posted a 70 on the last 18 holes, for a total score of 278. Jacobs had better health but a worse score—282.

Ken Venturi had completed the first comeback of his career by winning the U.S. Open, triumphing not only over his competition but over a remorseless heat that threatened to knock him out of the tournament completely.

Despite his weakened condition, Venturi still retained his sense of humor at the finish. When somebody commented on the advertising testimonials that would come his way as U.S. Open Champion, he grinned and said, "Maybe I'll be approached to do an ad for a salt company."

Following his dramatic win in the U.S. Open, many awards came Venturi's way. He was selected Sportsman of the Year by *Sports Illustrated,* Comeback of the Year by the Associated Press and Player of the Year by the Professional Golfers Association (PGA).

His physical ailments now a thing of the past, Venturi proved he still belonged in the upper echelon of pro golf. He went on to win the Insurance City Open and followed it by winning the American Golf Classic at Akron with a record score of 275, finishing off a fine year and placing his name high on the list of this country's most proficient golfers.

Then, at the top of his game again, his second illness struck.

Venturi's first indication that new trouble lay ahead of him came in October, 1964, while playing in Wentworth, England. The weather was chilly and damp, and Venturi's hands felt numb and cold. This did not concern him until after play was ended and he noticed that the skin on the tips of his fingers was peeling as far back as the nail. The skin was white and dead-looking, and his hands remained numb even after he was out of the bone-chilling weather.

Venturi thought that perhaps the cold-weather play was responsible, but next he went to Mexico, where it was warm, and the same trouble persisted. The fingers grew puffy, and the numbness caused him to lose his feel for the club. Worried, Venturi visited skin specialists, but none were sure what his trouble was.

The possibilities of this new illness frightened Venturi. In a game where so much depended on the feel of the club, Ken knew that numb fingers would ruin his game. Finally he contacted Dr. Robert Woods, the Los Angeles doctor who had treated Sandy Koufax. Dr. Woods made a frightening diagnosis. Venturi was the victim of a rare disease called Raynaud's phenomenon. In each wrist the transverse carpal ligament was compressing the median nerve, which controlled both movement and sensation in the fingers, and arteries carrying blood to the fingers were pinched. Eight fingers were affected by the disease; only his thumbs were normal.

Doctors advised Venturi to give up golf—at least temporarily—but the grit in Venturi wouldn't allow it. In January, 1965, he entered the Crosby Invitational with eight numb fingers. He used gloves and a hand warmer between shots, but they were of little help. He could hardly feel the club in his hands, and he found that, with his touch gone, he could barely control the club on drives or putts.

Venturi played three rounds of the Crosby tournament, shooting 81-75-77, but he did not qualify for the final round. Then came the 1965 United States Open, which he had won the year before, and Venturi felt an obligation to defend his championship. With no feeling in his hands, Venturi shot a wretched 81-79 and failed to survive the second-round cut.

It was a dismaying experience, and all Venturi could do was shake his head and sob, "How can I play? How can I ever play tournament golf again?"

On June 24, Ken Venturi entered Mayo Clinic for an operation to relieve his problem. Dr. Edward D. Henderson cut the transverse carpal ligaments, relieving the pressure on the median nerve and the pinched arteries. It took four months for Venturi to recover, during which time he was out of tournament golf.

His first appearance on a golf course following his operation was in Ryder Cup play at Southport, England, in October, 1965. Venturi knew that this was a supreme test, and he mustered all of the skills at his command. He did not win the tournament, but he was elated to find that he was at least capable of playing steady golf. He had not yet completely recovered all feeling in his fingers, but they were improving—and he was sure that his game was coming back.

In January, 1966, still not in top shape, he placed eighth and won $637 in the Los Angeles Open. Then, later in the same month, he entered San Francisco's $57,000 Lucky International Tournament—and this was the competition in which Ken Venturi made his second comeback from disaster complete.

Playing the best golf since his operation, Venturi fired back-to-back 68s the first two days of the tournament, using gloves and hand warmers again because the temperature was between 50 and 60 degrees. Then, gaining momentum, he shot a final round of 66 to win, collecting $8,500 as his first winner's check in two years.

It was one of the most satisfying tournaments of Venturi's career, for it signaled his second victory over misfortune and put him back among golfdom's elite. Plagued by illness, he had fought his way back twice in his career, showing a dogged determination that few men possess. After winning the Lucky International, Venturi might have been excused for exulting a little over his success. Instead, he capsuled his feelings in a few well-chosen words.

"It's nice," he said, "to be back among the players."

9

Ben Hogan . . .
the man who couldn't come back

It was the 1950 Los Angeles Open at Riviera, California, and the little man called Bantam Ben stood at the first tee, his jaw set in firm lines and his steel-gray eyes scanning the course. He should not have been there at all. Doctors had predicted that the little man—five-feet-ten and weighing less than 160 pounds—would never again walk normally, much less play golf. He had been assigned to the rocking chair at precisely the time when his golfing skills were at their height—and no one believed he could pick up the scattered remnants of his career and put them together again.

His name was Ben Hogan, and he was about to face the most crucial test of his life. Ten months ago he had been hovering between life and death, a physical wreck of a man who was expected to be a semi-invalid for the rest of his days. But a stubborn determination to continue his golfing career had pushed him into entering his name in the Los Angeles Open against an array of the best golfers of the time. Now, having taken the desperate plunge, he would either make a comeback that would astound the golfing world—or fail miserably and drop out of professional golf permanently.

Briefly, like a recurring nightmare, the memory of the accident came back to him, the terrible crash that had almost taken his life.

It was February 2, 1949, and Hogan and his wife, Valerie, were driving along a highway near Van Horn, Texas. It was a murky day, with a foglike haze hanging over the road. Suddenly, out of the thick mist, a huge bus loomed. It was coming directly toward them with its left wheels in Hogan's lane.

Hogan realized that a crash was unavoidable, and just before the violent collision he threw his body across the front seat to protect his wife from injury. Brakes screamed, and the vehicles crashed together. The immense weight of the bus shattered Hogan's car like an eggshell. The steering wheel was driven into the back of the driver's seat, where it would have impaled Hogan had he not thrown his body across his wife's. Valerie escaped serious injury, but Hogan was mangled terribly.

He suffered a broken collarbone, a shattered rib, a fracture of the pelvis and a broken left ankle.

Hogan was taken to a hospital in El Paso. When the extent of his injuries reached the newspapers, there was a sad shaking of heads among the reporters who had followed his career.

"Right now he's fighting for his life," said one writer. "But even if he wins that battle, he won't play golf any more."

The words were ominous, but they were undeniably logical. Golf is a meticulous game. Each shot must be not only carefully thought out, but executed with great skill. To display the kind of mastery that is required of the professionals, a man must keep all of his physical endowments honed to a fine edge. How could the horribly mangled Hogan ever hope to regain the skills he had possessed before the accident?

The doctors worked over the little man, and they set the bones and wrapped the lacerated legs in yards of bandage, and then they said, "Now we must wait." The sports world waited too, hanging on each bulletin issued by the hospital, wondering if the man some were calling the greatest golfer of all time could fight his way back—and knowing, instinctively, that it was asking the impossible.

Slowly Hogan's frail body began to heal, and just when it appeared he would at least live, he suffered a discouraging and dangerous relapse. A blood clot had formed in his battered leg. There was a danger that it would break away and reach his heart—and that would mean death.

The doctors did the only thing they could—they performed major surgery on one of his veins, sealing it off to prevent the clot from traveling to the heart. The operation saved Hogan's life but it did nothing for his leg, and it made a return to his golfing career even more unlikely. The doctors were certain now that Ben Hogan, his emaciated leg shrinking and bending abnormally, would never again walk as he had, and playing golf with his old skill—if at all—was virtually impossible.

For many days after the operation, Hogan was feverish and delirious. He lost weight alarmingly, and the little man became even littler. But a dogged determination to survive pulled him through, and a month after the operation he was sent home.

It was obvious to everyone that Ben Hogan was lucky just to be alive, and sports writers across the country wrote sad stories pronouncing the death knell of Hogan's career on the links. He was through, washed up, never again to excite the galleries with his mastery off the tees and his wizardry on the greens.

Hogan didn't believe the stories. In fact, each one he read

made him more determined to prove them wrong. At home he had to learn to walk all over again—short distances at first, then longer. His legs were stiff and swathed in bandages, and he hobbled around with great difficulty. He tired easily.

But, little by little, he strengthened his legs. As he gained back his weight and began to feel better, he went to a local golf course and practiced putting. He made no attempt to drive the ball from a tee. He was too weak for that.

But in time he did drive the ball—not well at first, but with improvement each time he tried.

During his long recovery period, Hogan had plenty of time to reflect on his career to date. He was now thirty-seven years old, having been born in the small town of Dublin, Texas, on August 13, 1912. His father had died when he was ten years old, and his mother moved the family to Fort Worth. At twelve years of age young Ben became a caddie at Glen Garden Country Club. At that time he had no thought of ever becoming a golfer; caddying paid 65 cents a round, and the family needed the money.

But young Ben succumbed to the lure of golf by watching other golfers play. The club gave an annual caddie tournament and, when he was fifteen, Ben entered it. He won it—a foretaste of what was to come.

In 1931, at nineteen years of age, Ben Hogan turned professional. This move was taken against the advice of older golfers. Hogan had a hook to his drives that wouldn't quit, and students of the game told him he would never make the grade as a pro. Nevertheless, he headed for Los Angeles to join the winter pro tour with only $100 in his pocket. He got nowhere in the tour and went broke besides. It wasn't until 1933 that he was able to try again. And again he failed.

Hogan then decided that he needed more practice before he could hope to compete at the professional level, and for the next four years he practiced incessantly.

In the meantime, young Hogan took on the responsibilities of a wife, and in 1936 and 1937 he made two more stabs at the pro game. Neither was marked with any great success.

When the 1938 winter tour started, Hogan was there, stubbornly trying his hand for the seventh year. In a tournament at Oakland, California, he experienced his first real success. He finished third and collected $385. That year, and in 1939, Hogan made only enough money to pay his expenses, but in 1940 he began to win with more regularity. In 1941 he had his biggest year so far, winning more than $18,000, and in 1942 he tied Byron Nelson in the Masters at Augusta, Georgia. In the play-off Nelson beat Hogan, but the important thing was that the little man was now on his way.

Then came another setback to Hogan's hopes. World War II started, and his budding career was abruptly interrupted. Hogan joined the Army Air Corps and did not play a serious round of golf until the war ended. Then, in 1946, he won his first major championship—the PGA title at Portland, Oregon. His earnings, $42,556 for the year, topped every golfer's in the land.

From that time, success fed on success. In 1948 he won the PGA again and added the United States Open at Riviera, California, to his collection of victories. In the U.S. Open he had four rounds of 67-72-68-69, for a total of 276—the best score ever posted in the National.

Then, in 1949, came the horrifying auto accident, followed by long months of practice in an effort to regain his skills. In the fall of that year, Hogan made an important decision.

He would enter the Los Angeles Open and subject himself to the acid test that would determine if he was fit any longer to play in the company of golfdom's great players.

The four-day tournament was an exhausting ordeal for Hogan. On the first day he staggered around on his weakened legs, posting a surprising first-round 73. The next two days he shot 69s. On the fourth day there was some question in even Hogan's mind if he could keep up the pace, but he forced his weary legs to carry him over the course as he shot another 69. His total score of 280 tied Sam Snead for the lead—and Hogan was forced to engage in a play-off to determine the winner.

Snead won the play-off, but Hogan had proved to himself the one thing he wanted to know—he could still play golf with the best of them!

Not everyone was as confident of this as Hogan. Golf-wise men shook their heads doubtfully. Sure, he had done well in the Los Angeles Open—remarkably well for a crippled man—but what would happen when he tried the United States Open? Here the competition would be much stiffer, and the 36-hole marathon that closed out the tournament on the final day would certainly be more than Hogan's stamina and gimpy legs could take.

The United States Open was held, that year, at the Merion Club outside Philadelphia. It was June, 1950, and Hogan felt that he had regained enough of his strength to face this ordeal with a good chance of winning. It didn't look as if this would be the case, however, for in the opening round Lee Mackey led with a record 64—and Hogan was eight strokes behind at 72.

On the second day the determined Hogan took a 69, and when the day ended he found himself just two strokes back.

This, in itself, was a remarkable spot for Hogan to be in, but on the third day of the tournament the cruelest test of all was awaiting any golfer whose physical endurance was not up to par. Everyone would have to play a double round —36 holes.

For Hogan's patched-up legs and battered body, this was torture at its worst. The game little man trudged around the course wearily, and little by little the strength drained out of him. Still his game did not falter. He managed a 72-74 that day, for a total score of 287, and when the trial was over he found himself in a three-way tie with Lloyd Mangrum and George Fazio.

Again he was faced with a grueling play-off.

This time Hogan was at his best. He carved out a brilliant 69, to win the tournament. It was such a substantial victory for the gallant little man that it convinced almost everyone that Hogan had, indeed, made his comeback and was destined to go on to greater things.

This he did. In 1951 he won his first Masters at Augusta, then took his second U.S. Open at Oakland Hills. In the Open he fired an amazing final round of 67. "That," he said, "was the finest round of golf of my career."

Hogan slipped slightly in 1952, when Julius Boros captured the Open at Dallas and Sam Snead grabbed the Masters. But he roared right back in 1953 and won both of them again—this time with ease. He set a record of 274 in the Masters, and won the Open at Oakmont, Pennsylvania, with a 283 that was six shots better than runner-up Sam Snead's score.

Despite his fine comeback record, however, Hogan still had a few detractors, as every athlete has. One who refused to believe what he had beheld said, "Okay, so he's won every major tournament in this country. But you can't say that he's won it all until he wins the British Open too. All the great golfers—Bobby Jones, Gene Sarazen, Walter Hagen—have won in Britain. Hogan will have to do it, too, before he can be numbered among the truly great."

Such remarks nettled Hogan, and he decided to show up his critics by entering the 1953 British Open at Carnoustie, on the east coast of Scotland. He went to Carnoustie early and practiced on the rugged course, studying every detail of it with the calm thoroughness of a scientist examining an insect under a microscope. He was fully aware that in the British Open he would encounter hazards unlike any he had ever experienced. The course was rough, full of holes, not well kept up. The greens were mushy and sticky—"like putty," as Hogan put it. Even the ball was different, the British ball being smaller than the American variety. And, on top of all that, there was the weather—almost perpetually foul, with heavy winds, slashing rain and bone-numbing cold.

As if that were not enough, he would also be facing the best golfers in the world.

The Scots, who are credited with originating the game of golf, watched Hogan's practice performances with deep admiration. They sensed what American golfers knew from experience, that on the course Hogan was a "loner"—cold and implacable and nerveless—and they nicknamed him the "Wee Ice Mon." They liked Hogan because he was small and gutsy, and by the time the British Open got under way, the Wee Ice Mon was a favorite of the Scots.

The favorite of the galleries is not always the favorite of the experts, though, and golf-wise men were convinced that Hogan had this time bitten off more than he could masticate.

His chances of winning the rugged British Open, they said, were nil.

Then, adding another hazard to the many, Ben Hogan developed a cold and fever just before the start of the tournament. He walked out on the course decked out in a couple of sweaters and rain gear as a cold, misty rain fell from a grayish sky. Despite illness, heavy weather, a troublesome course and a small ball, however, Hogan played the game with his usual precision and finished the first round with a creditable 73.

Even so, his 73 placed him three shots back of the leader, Frank Stranahan. So Hogan doggedly bettered his position in the second round by firing a 71. Stranahan, meanwhile, faded, and Hogan's score put him two back of Dai Rees and Eric Brown, two British Ryder Cup players.

During these two rounds the Scots followed their Wee Ice Mon around in the way that faithful dogs trail their masters. Almost to a man, they wanted Hogan to win. Perhaps they saw something in Hogan's brand of golf that the experts had overlooked, and that was his ability to place every shot in a favorable position from which to launch the next one. His thorough practice on the course before the British Open started had provided him with an asset the others lacked— he had "read" the course accurately; was familiar with its hazards, its pitfalls and its traps; and had mapped a plan to cope with all of them.

On the third round, still suffering from the cold, Hogan improved his score again, shooting a 70. That placed him in a tie with Roberto Di Vicenzo at 214.

The final round drew huge crowds of excited spectators. And the Wee Ice Mon put on a superb show. Exhibiting surprising power off the tees, meticulous pitch shots and accurate putting, he put together a score of 68 that gave him the British Open Championship by four strokes.

That was the crowning glory for Hogan. His name was now known all over the world, and he came home to be greeted by a ticker-tape parade on Broadway. There were no more doubters left; there could not be.

Hogan, exhibiting unbelievable courage, had come back from an accident that had nearly killed him and had apparently crippled him beyond the point where he could ever play championship golf again—and had won it all.

10
Glenn Cunningham . . .
miracle man of the track

Glenn Cunningham always did like to run. The boy from the plains of southwestern Kansas—who was to become one of the greatest mile runners of all time—used to delight in running to school every morning, to the grocery store for his parents or anywhere else his sturdy legs would carry him.

It was a cold winter morning in 1916, and seven-year-old Glenn was covering the distance between his farm home just outside Elkhart, Kansas, and the little school in town at a trot. With him was his brother, thirteen-year-old Floyd.

"We're late," Glenn said. "Maybe somebody beat us to it."

He was referring to a ritual that took place every morning. The first boy to reach the school was charged with the responsibility of lighting a fire in the schoolhouse stove so that the building would be warm by the time the other children arrived. Glenn and Floyd always prided themselves in being the fire starters.

When the boys let themselves into the school, they found that they were, indeed, the first to arrive. Floyd gathered some wood quickly and knelt down before the stove to fill the fire pot. Young Glenn picked up the can of kerosene which was used to prime the stove and handed it to Floyd. What neither boy knew was that someone the night before had made a mistake and had filled the can with gasoline instead of kerosene. Floyd poured the gasoline over the logs in the stove and tossed in a lighted match.

The result was an explosion that rocked the school and turned it into an inferno.

Floyd, who had been kneeling in front of the stove, was blown halfway across the room. Young Glenn, a few feet away, was knocked unconscious for a moment. When he came to, he found that the schoolroom was filled with smoke and flame and he could not see his brother at all.

"Floyd! Where are you?" he gasped.

There was no reply—just the angry crackling of burning wood and the billowing smoke and heat that filled the room.

Thinking his brother might have escaped from the building, Glenn staggered outside. But Floyd was not there. Desperately, Glenn went back into the blazing building. The heavy smoke blinded him, crept into his lungs, choked him. He could see nothing.

Suddenly he realized that his legs were burning. The flames had ignited his trousers and stockings, and he could feel the horrible pain as the fire crept up his legs.

Glenn rushed out of the building again and put out the flames in the snow. To his relief he saw that Floyd had also escaped from the building. Together they started for home. Both were badly burned. Both were in shock and in pain. But somehow they managed to make it home.

Floyd, who had taken the brunt of the explosion, died shortly after arriving home. A doctor was called to Glenn's bedside. He was burned over various parts of his body, but his legs were the most seriously injured. The doctor examined the boy carefully, his face grave. Glenn's parents, in grief over the death of their older son, watched anxiously. Finally the doctor straightened up. For a long time he did not speak. He was not certain Glenn would live, but he was sure of one thing. If he did, he would be a cripple. The youngster's left foot was so terribly burned that the transverse arch was completely destroyed. The tissues of his right leg were so severely seared that there was no hope that it would ever be normal again. It would shrivel and bend as scar tissue formed. There was even a chance that the leg would have to be amputated if it did not heal.

"I'm sorry to say this," the doctor told Glenn's parents, "but I must be truthful. The boy will probably survive, but even if the burns heal he will never walk normally again."

"He can't lose his legs," Glenn's mother said. "We'll pray for him."

His father nodded dumbly. Yes, they would pray for him. And maybe his legs would be saved. But even if they were, they would be of little use to him. This boy who loved to run so much would never run again. Never.

Sometimes doctors are wrong, or a miracle happens, or a person of great fortitude fights his way back from impossible odds. In Glenn Cunningham's case it is possible that all three of these events took place.

Slowly, very slowly, the burns on Glenn's legs healed. But in the healing process, scar tissue formed, the skin tightened and the legs became twisted and misshapen. The muscles were so badly injured that they did not respond to the healing in a normal way, and his legs were weak and powerless. For a long time he was forced to sit in a chair on the front porch, and the inactivity demoralized him.

"I don't want to sit here," he told the doctor one day. "I

want to walk and run. And I will—you just wait and see!"

The doctor smiled and patted his head. He had no confidence that Glenn would ever walk again. With crutches, maybe, but never without aid.

Glenn was just as certain that he *would* walk. *And* run. It was a dream he would not put aside.

His mother helped him to realize the dream. For months after the scar tissue had formed on his legs and the surface skin had hardened enough, she massaged his twisted legs. Her supple fingers kneaded the sore and strained muscles, and although the massaging was painful, Glenn put up with it. When his mother's arms and hands grew too tired to continue, Glenn would take over the massaging. Sometimes at night, in bed, he would massage his legs for hours.

For three years Glenn Cunningham walked on crutches. The daily massaging had helped him, but for a long time it seemed unlikely that it would help him to the point where he could walk unaided again.

Then, finally, the day came. When he was ten years old he tossed aside the crutches. The experience of walking without them was painful and discouraging. He hobbled and limped and staggered about. *But he walked!*

That was the beginning. From then on he walked without the crutches everywhere he went. He even tried to run, in a sort of disconnected, hippity-hop style.

One day he was limping around the front yard when the doctor drove up. The doctor stared in disbelief. He had not known that Glenn had discarded the crutches, and the sight of him walking astounded him.

"I told you I'd walk someday," Glenn said happily. "And I can run too." He hopped along to show the doctor.

"Had I not seen it with my own eyes, I would not have

believed it," he told Glenn's parents. "It's very encouraging, but I don't want to promise too much. It's possible that walking and running might restore some of the tissues in his legs. It's a remote possibility, but still a possibility."

Sometimes what seems like a miracle is actually brought about by a strong determination to succeed. This was the case with Glenn Cunningham. He insisted on running, despite stiffness and pain in his crooked legs. It took many years, but finally the pain began to lessen, the legs began to straighten a little and the muscles began to respond.

Glenn still limped when he entered high school, but he had forced himself to run and he could now move along with surprising efficiency. In a move that was typical of his enthusiasm for running, Glenn joined the high school track team.

A year or so later he entered a mile race—*and won it!*

When Glenn graduated from high school, he went to the University of Kansas on an athletic scholarship. Brutus Hamilton, track coach at Kansas, had lured Glenn to the U of K after seeing him run in high school. Hamilton was high on the boy. "He just might turn out to be the greatest mile runner this country has ever seen," he said. "He has the speed, the stamina—and he certainly has the dedication."

Glenn Cunningham was a sophomore at the university in 1931 when a new world record for the mile was set by Jules Ladoumegue, a Frenchman. The time was 4:09.2. Glenn was not yet good enough to challenge that speed, but in an NCAA meet shortly after, he came close to it by setting a new American record, covering the mile in 4:11.1.

That feat put his name in the sports pages of every newspaper in the country.

From that time on, Glenn Cunningham was consistently

in the news. People who had never taken an interest in track-and-field events became fascinated by his endeavors. Almost every race he ran was headline news, and Cunningham quickly became a towering figure in racing.

The 1932 Olympics were held in Los Angeles, and Glenn was chosen to represent the United States on its Olympic Team. Up against the best competition in the world, Glenn placed fourth in the metric mile, a distance of 1,500 meters. In 1933 he continued to win in important track meets and was awarded the Sullivan Trophy as the year's top amateur athlete.

But it seemed that every time Glenn Cunningham came close to setting a record in the mile run, somebody else lowered the time a little more. In 1934 a New Zealander, John E. Lovelock, posted a new world record of 4:07.6. That gave Glenn a new goal to shoot at.

Glenn Cunningham's only real competition in this country came from a young man named Bill Bonthron, who did his running for Princeton University. The two met head-on in 1934 in a mile race that has gone down in track history as one of the most dramatic—and possibly the best race Glenn Cunningham ever ran.

The race was run at Princeton's Palmer Stadium on June 16, 1934, and more than 25,000 people turned out to see the top two mile runners in the land in what was billed as a "classic clash." To Cunningham this was a supreme test, and he could not help but look down at his permanently scarred legs and think of how far they had taken him since that horrifying day when the school fire had turned him into a cripple. Now he hoped they would take him just a little farther and permit him to beat Bonthron and—just maybe— set a new world record.

But there was no time for wishful thinking. Glenn was at

the starting line with Gene Venzke, a miler from the University of Pennsylvania, and Bonthron—a three-man race that had the crowd on the edge of their seats even before it began. It was a Princeton crowd, of course, and Bonthron was the favorite. Glenn knew he would hear few cheers no matter what he did, but he wanted to win this race against his greatest foe more than any in which he had participated.

The starting gun sounded, and the three runners took off. Venzke, with long strides, took the lead. Glenn Cunningham was second and Bonthron third. All three fell into the steady, flowing, strength-conserving stride of the miler who knows that the distance is great and that speed must be rationed.

Venzke retained the lead for the first quarter mile, setting a pace just brisk enough to force the two men behind him to extend themselves a little. In the second quarter, though, Glenn noticed that Venzke had slowed his pace to conserve energy for the finish. Glenn went around him quickly to take the lead.

Bonthron, knowing that Cunningham was the man to beat, also passed Venzke. He was not about to let Glenn gain an insurmountable lead on him.

The three runners stayed in this position, closely bunched, until the half-mile mark was reached.

It was just after the completion of the half mile that Glenn embarked on some dangerous strategy. He increased his speed suddenly and began to open up the distance between himself and his two rivals. Bonthron couldn't understand it. This was suicide. You never made this kind of move with a half mile to go. In the last quarter, yes—but not with half a mile yet to run. Cunningham would burn himself out too early and be running last by the time the finish line loomed.

But Cunningham pulled away, increasing his lead to ten

yards, then fifteen. Finally, Bonthron panicked. He started out after the fleeing Cunningham, stepping up his own speed. He had no choice. He could not let Cunningham get a decisive lead on him. He had to stay close. If they were going to burn themselves out before the finish, they would have to burn together!

But despite Bonthron's increased speed, Cunningham kept pulling away. Glenn was unstoppable now. His lead over Bonthron crept up to twenty yards, then thirty. Venzke fell far behind. And at last the pro-Bonthron crowd realized that Cunningham was running the greatest mile of his career, and they cheered him lustily as he crossed the finish line— more than forty yards ahead of Bonthron!

In his most brilliant race, Glenn Cunningham had set a new world record, beating Lovelock's mark of 4:07.6 with an amazing 4:06.7. The record for the mile had been returned to America on the winged feet—and battered legs—of Glenn Cunningham.

This dramatic victory might have marked the end of Glenn Cunningham's career, except for one thing. About this time people were beginning to wonder if, someday, someone might run the mile in less than four minutes. For years the four-minute mile had been thought to be an impossible goal. Influential men in track and field pronounced it an impossibility. Many felt that the human heart would give out under the unceasing pressure a four-minute mile would impose on a runner. But there were a few who thought that man was on the threshold of the four-minute mile, and that Cunningham's record time of 4:06.7 proved that it could be done.

Cunningham wasn't sure whether the four-minute mile could be run or not, but in 1938 he decided to give it a try. He traveled to Dartmouth, where a brand new track gave him a chance to crack the goal that no one had yet achieved. He had several other runners pace him—that is, they ran ahead of him, setting a fast pace and forcing Cunningham to keep up with them. Each runner ran a certain distance and then dropped out, letting a fresh runner take over. Cunningham, pushing himself to the limit to keep pace with the faster runners, electrified the world of track by running the mile in 4:04.4!

Because this was not a race in the true sense, the record was not recognized, but the very fact that Cunningham had reduced the time to just over four minutes changed the minds of many track followers. Perhaps the four-minute mile was possible after all! If a man troubled by bad legs throughout his career could set a mark of 4:04.4, couldn't some future runner with sturdier legs crack the four-minute barrier?

As it turned out, it was sixteen years before the mile was run in less than four minutes. On May 6, 1954, an Englishman named Roger Bannister covered the distance at Oxford in an official time of 3:59.4.

The assault on the four-minute mile had finally ended, and Bannister became one of the great names in track. But it was Cunningham who, before retiring from racing in 1940, had come closest to that goal—and had convinced others that it could be done.

Glenn Cunningham had fought his way back from a crippling accident that had threatened to put him in a wheel chair for life to set the stage for ultimate victory over the "impossible" four-minute mile—and had become one of the greatest and most memorable athletes of our times.

11

Bob Cousy . . .
pro basketball's wee wizard

Of all the sports played by man, basketball offers the biggest challenge to the little man. This is a game of giants. Men who tower six-feet-ten, six-eleven or seven feet are commonplace. The over-seven-footer is not unusual.

Since the primary object of the game is to toss a ball through a hoop stationed ten feet above a gymnasium floor, it is obvious that the tall man has a distinct advantage over the smaller player. A seven-footer, by leaping and stretching his arm above his head, can easily dunk the ball into the basket at close range.

When coaches and scouts search out players for their teams, they look for the big man. It is true that they are also interested in a man who can handle the ball well, has an unerring eye when he shoots at the basket and is quick and alert and shifty. If a little man has these talents, he has a little man's chance to make the grade. If a tall man has them, he is in.

There is a saying in sports that "a good big man can beat a good little man every time," and this is certainly true in basketball. At least, it is true most of the time. But exceptions do occur, and a notable one took place in 1950 when a young man of miniature-to-medium size joined the Boston Celtics professional basketball team.

His name was Bob Cousy. And what he did in pro basketball was so unbelievable that it deserves special emphasis in the history of the game.

Robert Joseph Cousy was born on August 9, 1928, in a section of New York City called Yorkville. His father, Joseph, was a native of Alsace-Lorraine and his mother, Juliette, an American citizen, but the couple had lived in France until six months before Bob's birth and French was spoken in their home. Young Bob did not learn to speak English until he started to attend school.

The family lived on New York's East Side until Bob was eleven years old. During those days he played all the street games of New York's slum areas—stickball, stoopball and other games that could be played in limited space. He learned to swim in the East River, where filth in the form of coal dust and garbage made the experience less than ideal.

With Bob approaching twelve years of age, the family moved to St. Albans in Queens County. This was a suburban area with more space for recreational activities, and Bob Cousy began to play baseball and handball in a playground near his home. This introduction to sports almost came to a halt, though, when young Bob fell from a tree and broke his right arm.

It was a nasty blow for an active youngster, but Bob showed the kind of courage at this point that was to be important to him throughout life. He simply continued playing handball and baseball—left-handed. The experience provided him with a kind of ambidexterity that was later to work to his advantage in basketball.

Bob Cousy discovered basketball at the age of thirteen, and soon realized that basketball was *his* game. He had a natural talent for it, and there was no greater thrill than dribbling his way through a group of several youngsters on the playground court and scoring on a well-executed lay-up. When he entered Andrew Jackson High School in Queens, he immediately went out for freshman basketball, and it was at this point that he received a rude awakening.

He failed to make the team.

The reason was obvious. There was a large group of boys out for the team, and most of them were taller than Bob. Young Cousy stood only five-feet-eight, and Coach Lew Grummond overlooked him completely. Grummond had his mind set on taller boys, and he failed even to notice Cousy.

When Bob tried out for basketball again in his sophomore year, he again was shunted aside. Discouraged but not beaten, Bob Cousy joined amateur teams outside of school and continued to play basketball.

One night Coach Grummond was watching an amateur game in which Cousy was performing well, and he suddenly realized that this talented young man actually attended Andrew Jackson High School. In his junior year, when Bob again tried out for the high school team, he received special attention from the coach. This time he made the grade.

Bob Cousy didn't wait long to convince Grummond that he had made a good decision. In his first varsity game he scored 28 points and then led Jackson High to the Queens championship. As a senior he was again the key man in leading Jackson High to the championship, and in the process

Cousy won the scoring title. At the conclusion of his senior year, he was named captain of New York City's All-Scholastic five.

Despite his fine record in high school, Bob Cousy was not overwhelmed by collegiate scholarship offers. College recruiters made the same mistake Grummond had made—they considered Cousy "too small" to play basketball at the college level. Only two schools showed mild interest in him. One was Boston College, the other the College of the Holy Cross at Worcester, Massachusetts. Cousy decided to attend Holy Cross.

The year was 1946 and, under a World War II ruling, freshmen were eligible to play on the varsity team. Cousy, exhibiting a flair for ball handling and shooting, made the team, but he did not make the starting lineup. The taller players, as usual, were favored.

Discouraged by this stubborn preference for tall players, Cousy tried all the harder to make an impression on those few occasions when he was sent out on the court. He showed a talent for dribbling the ball with either hand, passing off to teammates without even looking (sometimes passing the ball behind his own back in the tricky manner of the Harlem Globetrotters) and scoring with accurate one-handed jump shots and push shots. He was so good that even the tall-man-oriented coach could not help but admire him. So, by the time his sophomore year rolled around, Bob Cousy found himself a member of the starting lineup.

Cousy, given his chance, immediately made his mark in collegiate ball. As a sophomore, he led Holy Cross into the semifinals of the NCAA tournament in 1948. Then he went on to become the highest scorer in Holy Cross history and was named All-American in his senior year.

Cousy graduated from college in June, 1950, with a B.S. degree in business administration. He had high hopes that the professional Boston Celtics would choose him in the annual college draft of players, but they passed him by in the first round. Instead, he was picked up by a Midwest team called Tri-Cities (a three-part team made up of Rock Island and Moline, Illinois, and Davenport, Iowa).

What happened after that had Cousy's head buzzing. Before Bob could even report to his new team, Tri-Cities traded him to a Chicago outfit called the Stags. But, even before the training camp opened, the Stags declared themselves bankrupt and dropped out of the league. It was decided that the Stags' players would be turned over to the other teams in the league.

The distribution plan went well until it reached the last three names on the list—Andy Phillips, Max Zaslofsky and Bob Cousy. These players were to be divided between the Boston Celtics, New York Knickerbockers and Philadelphia Warriors. A great hassle occurred. All three teams wanted Zaslofsky; Phillips was the second choice. Rookie Bob Cousy was last.

When the teams failed to come to any agreement, it was decided that they would draw names out of a hat. The Boston Celtics ended up with Cousy—a great break for Bob but one that the Celtics at the time did not consider exactly enchanting.

Red Auerbach was coach of the Celtics when Cousy joined the team, and it wasn't long before he began to realize that his new player had unusual talent. He was the kind of flashy player who brought fans to the game in droves. He was blessed with split-second reflexes, alertness and peripheral vision that permitted him to see teammates out of the corners of his eyes. He would dribble the ball down the floor, fake a shot at the basket and then pass the ball to a teammate on his right or left without turning his head, sometimes faking a shot with his right hand to pull a defender in that direction, then quickly shifting the ball to his left hand and sinking the basket.

This kind of razzle-dazzle kept opposing teams completely off balance, and when his first season (1950-51) was over, "The Cooz," as he came to be known, was voted the National Basketball Association Rookie of the Year.

Although Cousy was a good scorer, his real value to the Celtics was his talent as a playmaker. His ball-handling knack made him the league's top assist man for eight seasons in a row (an assist being recorded when a pass permits another man to score). His tricky style of play made it possible for him to either move in for a shot or pass off, and he passed off to a teammate more often than he tried to score.

For six years the Celtics failed to win a championship, but Cousy's personal popularity grew despite the failure of the team. In 1955 President Eisenhower invited him and several other star athletes to the White House for luncheon. In 1956 Boston's Junior Chamber of Commerce named him one of Greater Boston's Outstanding Young Men. In 1957 the National Basketball Association voted him Most Valuable Player. So it went for Cousy, who was now established as one of the great players of the game.

In the 1956-57 season the Boston Celtics finally won the Eastern Division championship, with the help of Cousy and a sensational rookie named Bill Russell. They went on to win the play-off against the St. Louis Hawks in a tense seven-game series.

That was the beginning of a dynasty for the Celtics. The

next year (1957-58), the St. Louis Hawks won the NBA championship from the Celtics four games to two. But in the next four years (1958-59, 1959-60, 1960-61, 1961-62) Boston took the NBA title.

By this time Bob Cousy had reached the ripe old age of thirty-four and had decided to play one more year of professional ball before shifting to coaching college basketball. In his last year (1962-63) the Celtics again won the Eastern Division title after a stiff struggle, then went on to defeat Cincinnati in the semifinals of the championship play-offs. The victory earned them the right to take on the Los Angeles Lakers for the National Basketball Association crown, and the experts, this time, were almost unanimously picking the Lakers to end the Celtics' grip on the title.

With his retirement from the game so close, Cousy was particularly anxious to win the championship. It would be a nice way to bow out, he thought. And, the way the Celtics started against the Lakers, it looked like a shoo-in. They won three of the first four games played and needed only one more to grab the title.

But the Lakers delayed Cousy's big moment by winning the fifth game at Boston Gardens, and the two teams traveled to Los Angeles for the sixth contest.

This game proved, beyond any doubt, the value of Bob Cousy to the Celtics. With him, they were a ball team; without him, they stumbled.

The Celtics had little trouble with the Lakers in the first half, building up a 14-point lead at half time, and it looked as if they were well on their way to putting a lock on the championship. Coming back on the court after the rest period, the Celtics held their lead through the third quarter. Then, in the fourth, disaster loomed.

Cousy was bringing the ball down the court, dribbling as he kept his eyes alertly focused on the Lakers' defensive maneuvering. Then suddenly, for what appeared to be no reason whatever, Cousy twisted his ankle and collapsed to the hardwood floor in a heap. He lay there, grimacing with pain, and the Celtics' trainer rushed out on the floor. Minutes later he was helping Cousy from the court to the bench.

To say that the Celtics missed Cousy would be putting it mildly. They were virtually helpless without him. With Cousy squirming on the sidelines, the Celtics fell apart. Suddenly their defense faltered, and they became a bungling, inept team on offense. The Lakers, seeing their chance, rallied. The Celtics' lead began to fade. It slipped from ten points to seven, then six.

Cousy fidgeted on the bench. It wasn't only his ankle that pained him. He was feeling the agony of seeing a comfortable lead dwindle away.

"Freeze my ankle," he said to the trainer. "I can go back in the game."

The trainer shook his head. The lead continued to shrink. Six points, four, two. The Celtics teetered on the brink of a humiliating defeat.

"Freeze the ankle!" Cousy repeated.

Suddenly the Lakers were only one point behind the staggering Celtics, and the clock showed there were still two minutes to play. Plenty of time for the Lakers to pull ahead and wrap up the game.

With time ticking away and the Celtics still clinging to their precarious one-point lead, the trainer finally "froze" Cousy's ankle. The pain subsided miraculously and, with a signal from the coach, he trotted back on the court.

Cousy was not sure that he could help the Celtics in a

physical sense. But he reasoned rightly about one thing. His presence would inspire them and maybe, in that case, they would be able to hang on and emerge the victor.

It worked just that way. With Cousy back in the game, the Celtic defense suddenly tightened. The Lakers tried desperately to work the ball down the court for an easy lay-up that would put them ahead, but they were stopped by the suddenly improved defense of the Celtics. Working the ball around the Celtics' defensive perimeter, the Lakers found it impossible to move in for a close shot.

Then a defensive play occurred that turned the game around. Cousy himself was not involved, but his presence pushed a teammate, Tom Heinsohn, to new heights when he stole a pass from the Lakers and raced in for an easy lay-up that gave the Celtics a three-point edge.

The Celtics held on then, grimly, and when the buzzer sounded the end of the game, the scoreboard read Celtics 112, Lakers 109.

Bob Cousy had realized his ambition to bow out with a victory. More than that, the kid from New York's East Side— who had been too small to play high school basketball, too small to play in college and too small to make the pros— had overcome his so-called handicap to become one of the greatest and most memorable players of the game. He had proved that there was a place even in basketball for a good little man.

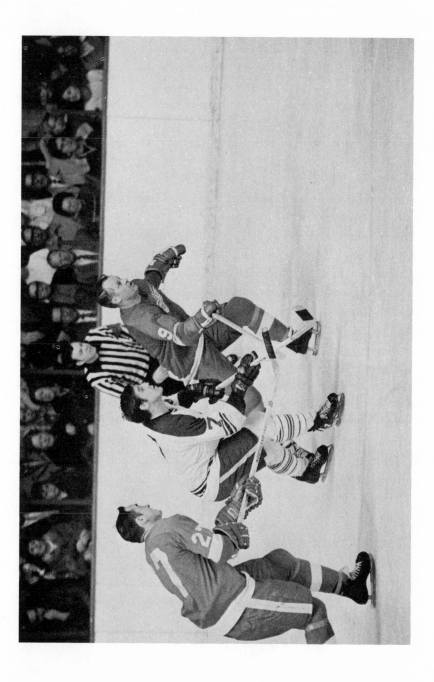

12

Gordie Howe . . .
greatest hockey player of all time

It was March 28, 1950, and a capacity crowd of 13,659 fans had shoved their way into Detroit's Olympia Stadium to watch the Red Wings battle the Toronto Maple Leafs in the first game of the 1949-50 Stanley Cup play-offs. The Wings were favored to take Toronto apart in the series, despite the fact that Toronto had won the Stanley Cup three years in a row and had whipped the Red Wings eleven straight times in the process.

There were several reasons for Red Wing optimism. Detroit had enjoyed a highly successful season, finishing 14 games ahead of Toronto in the final National Hockey League standings. Their famous Production Line of Sid Abel, Ted Lindsay and Gordie Howe had forged a great scoring year—215 points on 92 goals and 123 assists. But most important of all was the fact that the twenty-two-year-old Gordie Howe, playing his fourth season at right wing, had suddenly blossomed, after three unimpressive years, into one of the most feared forwards in the league. He had accounted for 68 of

137

the points scored by the Production Line, and his high-caliber play marked him as a coming great.

Gordie Howe was just under six feet tall and weighed 200 pounds. Away from the game he was a shy, easygoing and somewhat awkward young man, but on the ice he was a raging terror. He could deliver bone-shattering body checks, and his clever stick handling was next to unbelievable. He skated with long, easy strides that made him look slow, but he always got where he was going before anyone else. As for his scoring ability, there was no goalie in the league who relished facing his withering shots on goal.

But on this particular night neither Gordie Howe nor the other two members of the Red Wings' high-scoring line could make much of a dent in the Maple Leafs' defense. Toronto was known around the league for its roughhouse tactics, and in defending their goal they subjected the Wings to bruising punishment all evening. By the time the final period rolled around, the score indicated the extent to which Toronto had throttled the sorely pressed Red Wings.

It was Toronto Maple Leafs 4, Detroit Red Wings 0.

That was bad enough to send both the Red Wings and their fans home in a depressed state, but what happened in the final period was pure tragedy.

About halfway through the third stanza, Ted (Teeder) Kennedy, the Toronto captain, trapped the puck at center ice and set out at high speed along the boards toward the Red Wing goal. Gordie Howe, under such circumstances, had a one-track mind—stop him! With long strides he swept across the rink and attempted to pin Kennedy to the boards. Had he succeeded, he might have flattened Kennedy like a pancake.

But this time it didn't work. The agile Kennedy stopped short just as Howe threw the check. Losing his balance, Gordie sailed in front of Kennedy and crashed head-first into the boards. The sickening thud could be heard all over the stadium—the kind of dull thunk that hockey fans have come to associate with serious injury.

Gordie Howe lay semiconscious on the ice, his face splashed with blood.

The game erupted in a near-brawl. Red Wing players accused Kennedy of deliberately injuring Howe by poking the butt end of his hockey stick in Gordie's face as he flew by. Kennedy stoutly denied it. The argument was unimportant as far as Howe was concerned, for he was carried from the rink on a stretcher while the players of both teams milled around him in angry confusion.

Howe was dimly aware of being carried off the ice, of a fast ride in an ambulance with a siren wailing, of his careful transfer to a hospital bed. Through a gauzelike haze he could see white-clad nurses fluttering about and Dr. Charles L. Tomsu, the team physician, bending over him. Howe had suffered severe multiple injuries—a cut eyeball, lacerated face, broken nose, broken cheekbone and a brain concussion.

About midnight Dr. Tomsu realized that a growing pressure on the brain was developing. He immediately called in Dr. Frederic Schreiber, a brain specialist, for consultation. It was agreed that a delicate operation—the drilling of a hole in the skull—would have to be performed to remove the pressure. Otherwise, Howe was in danger of losing his life.

At one o'clock in the morning, long after the Red Wings

had taken a 5-0 drubbing from the Leafs, Howe was wheeled into the hall towards the operating room. Jack Adams, the irascible coach of the Red Wings, walked beside him, his fiery nature completely subdued by the accident. Howe, still only half conscious, smiled weakly.

"I'm sorry I couldn't help you more tonight," he mumbled.

Adams had no answer. He watched silently as they wheeled Howe into the clinically white operating room and closed the door behind them. The doctors had been candid. They did not know if Howe would ever play hockey again. They did not even know if he would live.

Adams forced back tears. It was he who had recognized the vast potential of Gordie Howe. It was he who had signed him to a Red Wing contract. It was he who had predicted that Howe would become one of the greats of the game—perhaps the greatest ever.

Now it looked as if the young man's career, and maybe his life, was at an end.

Gordon (Gordie) Howe was born March 31, 1928, in Floral, Saskatchewan, a granary depot on the outskirts of Saskatoon, deep in the wheat belt of central Canada. He was the fourth of nine children born to Albert and Katherine Howe, and the only one destined to become a superstar in Canada's unique and violent sport.

When Gordie was only a few months old, the Howe family moved to a two-story frame-and-shingle house on Avenue L North in Saskatoon, where Gordie's father took a job running a garage and later became a maintenance superintendent for the city. While the elder Howe was busy supporting his rapidly expanding family, Gordie was busy growing up into a strapping youngster who was always a little bigger—and a little more awkward—than boys the same age. This awkwardness was noticeable in everything Gordie did, with one exception—skating. With a pair of ice skates on his feet, he could skim over a glassy surface with grace and speed.

Gordie received his first pair of skates in the Depression year of 1934 when a woman called at the Howe home and offered to sell a sack of clothing and other odds and ends for fifty cents. Mrs. Howe bought the sack, and Gordie immediately dug out an old pair of skates. His eyes lit up.

"Can I have them, Ma?" he asked. "Can I?"

"They're too big for you," his mother said.

"I'll fill them with socks," Gordie replied.

He put on four pairs of socks, and they were still too big for him; but they were his skates, and he was proud of them. He learned to skate on them with astonishing ease, and from then on he either skated or played hockey every spare moment of his time.

Gordie Howe attended Westmount and King George grade schools, but he was often tired out by the time he reported for his morning classes. The reason was that he would get up at six o'clock in the morning and play hockey before reporting to school—even when the weather was 25 to 50 degrees below zero. While he was at King George he joined the King George Athletic Club's midget hockey team, which was coached by a woman named Mrs. Bert Hodges. It was his first taste of organized play.

By the time Gordie reached the age of fifteen, he was a big, powerful, hard-muscled kid with a budding hockey talent. His skills on the ice had matured rapidly. He had developed the long-striding, easygoing skating style that was to become his trademark. His precocious stick handling had become pure wizardry, permitting him to "rag" the puck endlessly as other players tried vainly to take it away from him. And his ability to hit an open corner of the net with his shots on goal had become uncannily accurate.

None of this went unnoticed by hockey scouts. During the summer following Gordie's fifteenth birthday, Fred McCorry, a scout for the New York Rangers, invited him to report to the Rangers' training camp in Winnipeg for a tryout.

The thrill of reporting to the training camp of a major-league hockey club filled Gordie with hope, but the actual experience was a disaster. Because he was shy and withdrawn, the older players kidded him unmercifully, stole his plate of food at the training table and continually embarrassed him. They took a perverse delight in making him uncomfortable.

"Where you from, kid?" they'd ask.

"Saskatoon," Gordie would reply.

"Where's that?"

"In Saskatchewan."

"Saskatoon, Saskatchewan? You're kidding. There ain't no such place."

"Yes there is," Gordie would insist.

"What is it near?"

"Floral."

"Floral? Where's that?"

"Near Saskatoon."

"In Saskatchewan?"

"Yeah."

Worst of all, from Gordie's viewpoint, was the fact that the Ranger brass paid little attention to him, and finally he returned home in disappointment. He was convinced he would never make it in big-time hockey.

But the next fall Fred Pinckney, a scout for the Detroit Red Wings who had been watching Gordie, asked him to report for a tryout at the Detroit training camp in Windsor, Ontario. The coach of the Red Wings at the time was the tough and crusty Jack Adams. Adams had an unerring eye for hockey talent, and he spotted Gordie at once as a comer. He signed Gordie to a $4,000 contract and sent him to the Red Wings' Junior A club in Galt, Ontario.

Just when Gordie thought he was on the way, another barrier to his success rose before him. Galt was an eastern city in Canada, and Saskatoon was in the west. League rules specified that no western Canada player could perform with an eastern team; Gordie Howe was declared ineligible and was forced to sit out a full year while he watched his Galt teammates play from the stands.

The Red Wings corrected their mistake the next year by sending Gordie to their Omaha team in the United States Hockey League. This was pretty fast company for a seventeen-year-old, but Gordie was an immediate success, getting 48 points on 22 goals and 26 assists for the season. That performance earned him a promotion, and the next year (the 1946-47 season) Gordie was a member of the Detroit Red Wings.

Gordie Howe was not exactly a ball of fire in his first year of National Hockey League play. He scored only seven goals and had 15 assists, for a meager 22 points. He improved in 1947-48, when he doubled his total points on 16 goals and 28 assists. But in his third year he fell back to 12 goals and 25 assists, for a point total of 37.

Although Gordie's three-year record was not impressive, Jack Adams never lost faith in him. He saw in Gordie a latent talent such as few young men possessed. "He'll explode one of these seasons," Adams predicted, "and he'll become one of the greatest players ever. Mark my words."

One of Gordie's worst faults in those first three years was his tendency to get into fights. He seemed to think that he had to show Adams his ability to take care of himself on the ice, and Adams finally took him aside one day and corrected that impression.

"Okay, Gordie," he said. "You've convinced me you can lick anybody in the league. But nobody ever scored a goal while sitting in the penalty box. Now show me you can play hockey."

Gordie showed him. Holding his temper in check and concentrating on the game, young Howe—just twenty-two years old—demonstrated his real ability the following year (1949-50). He played in 70 games and racked up 35 goals and 33 assists, for 68 points, and proved unmistakably that he had arrived as a full-fledged major-league hockey player.

Then, in the Stanley Cup play-offs with the Toronto Maple Leafs that same year, he suffered the serious injury that sent him to the hospital for a brain operation—and the word was out that, even if he lived, he might never play hockey again.

Gordie Howe had been cruelly cut down just at the time when he had exploded, as Jack Adams had predicted, into a star performer.

But Gordie Howe survived the operation to remove pressure from his brain, and during the off-season he recovered fully from the multiple injuries he had suffered. Still, the

Red Wing front office worried about their brilliant young
star. An injury as serious as the one Gordie had suffered
could turn a man to mush inside. It could take the fire out
of him and reduce him to impotency, and Jack Adams and
other front-office personnel were asking themselves two important questions. Would Gordie ever again body-check with
the same savage recklessness? Or would he be inclined to
avoid body contact, to shy away from roughing it up with
opposing players? If he turned overly cautious, it would take
a lot away from his playing style, and he would become a
run-of-the-mill hockey player instead of the great star he
promised to be.

Gordie Howe answered these questions in the only way he
knew how—on the ice. Playing without a trace of fear or
caution throughout the 1950-51 season, Gordie racked up
43 goals and 43 assists, for a total of 86 points—enough to
lead the league in both goals scored and total points. It was
a fantastic comeback year for Gordie, and it proved he had
lost none of his grit or determination. It also proved that
he was, indeed, a major star who would have to be reckoned
with for many years to come.

From that season on there was no stopping the kid from
Saskatoon. Season after season, he stood out among all
hockey players like a beacon on a black night. Before long,
Jack Adams was calling him the "greatest hockey player
of all time" and the New York Rangers' Muzz Patrick was
reluctantly agreeing with him. In fact, virtually everyone
in the National Hockey League was looking with awe at
Gordie Howe—especially the players who had to oppose
him on the ice. They knew, better than anyone, what it was

to cope with this hard-skating, straight-shooting, rugged and sometimes mean player.

At the time that Howe was having some of his greatest years, another NHL player was also making headlines. He was the great Maurice (the Rocket) Richard, of the Montreal Canadians. Known as the Flying Frenchman, Richard was one of the finest goal scorers in the history of the game. His great scoring talent and Gordie's all-around offensive-defensive ability were provoking some lively discussions around the league. The question bandied about was: Who is the best?

Actually, it was foolish to try to compare the two players because they were complete opposites. Richard was a fiery, spectacular player. No one ever doubted that he was great, because it showed in every move he made. He was a showman as well as a hockey player, a performer who could lift the crowd out of its seats with his flashy style of play. Gordie Howe, on the other hand, was almost languid in his playing style. His greatness was hidden in an easygoing manner and an effortless talent that made every play look easy. His long, graceful skating stride made him look considerably slower than his opponents, but he always managed to be where the puck was. Ted Lindsay, his Red Wing teammate, put it well. "I always have to work twice as hard and put out ten times as much effort to do what Gordie does easily," he said.

An example of Howe's relaxed style of play occurred one memorable night in a game with the Chicago Black Hawks. It was the final period of play, and the Red Wings were trailing by one goal. The seconds on the clock were ticking away when Howe got the puck inside the enemy blue line. Jack Adams, highly excited, yelled across the ice.

"Shoot, Gordie, shoot!"

But Howe took his time about it. He stick-handled the puck with ease as he skated across the rink from one wing position to the other. The seconds kept ticking away—twenty, fifteen, ten, five. Still Gordie toyed with the puck. Finally, moving quickly around a defense man, Howe drilled the shot toward the net. The Chicago goalie hit the ice to block the shot. He was too late: the puck went into the net just as the buzzer sounded to end the game!

In the dressing room the distraught Adams asked Howe why he had waited so long. Gordie smiled sheepishly.

"I guess I just wanted to make sure," he drawled.

It's easy to see why Gordie wore the mantle of greatness by analyzing his many talents. First, Howe had a calm disposition. It was impossible to ruffle him in tight situations. He played every game, regardless of the score or its importance, with the workmanlike precision of a robot and never panicked under pressure. But this casual demeanor was not to be taken for cowardice. He could be transformed from a languid performer into a violent buzz saw if somebody roughed him unnecessarily. As one player put it, "You can rough Howe up and he won't retaliate right away. He'll just skate away as if nothing happened. But a little while later he'll get his chance in a mix-up on the ice, and all of a sudden you'll skate away bleeding without knowing how it happened."

Fine reflexes and coordination were other capabilities that put Howe in a class by himself. His stick handling was unequaled by any other player, and on top of this delicate skill was the fact that he was ambidextrous—he could shoot the puck either right- or left-handed, shifting his hands on the stick—which made him a rarity seldom seen.

Besides all this, Howe was physically tough. During his long career he suffered more than his share of injuries, but none ever stopped him for long. He suffered the loss of two front teeth, had operations on both knees, gashed his thigh, dislocated his shoulder, tore his rib cartilages, broke his nose several times and his wrist once and was almost killed in the 1949-50 play-offs with the Toronto Maple Leafs when he suffered the brain injury. Still, he missed comparatively few games and, in 1952-53, when he scored 95 points that set a scoring record at the time, he played 16 games with a broken right wrist encased in a clumsy cast!

Gordie was always philosophical about injuries and considered them merely a part of his trade. Commenting on the subject one time, he said casually, "One year I had fifty stitches in my face. That was a bad year. Another time I had only ten. That was a good year."

Howe probably became recognized as a true superstar from the 1951-52 season through the 1954-55 campaign, when the Red Wings dominated the National Hockey League. In 1951-52 the Red Wings ran away with the National Hockey League race and then swept the Stanley Cup play-offs in eight straight games—the first time in hockey history this had been accomplished. They won both the league championship and the Stanley Cup in 1953-54 and in 1954-55, too. Gordie Howe, contributing immensely to this record, scored 86, 95 and 81 points during those big years.

All through those years the intense rivalry between Gordie Howe and "Rocket" Richard continued, but by the 1960s more and more hockey experts were supporting Howe as the "greatest player." There was no doubt that Richard was one of the great scorers of the game, but he had little talent for defense. Howe, on the other hand, was the best all-around player, having both offensive and defensive abilities.

And then, on November 10, 1963, Howe even took the scoring title away from Richard.

The great Rocket had retired from the game in 1960 with a National Hockey League record of 544 goals in his career. Gordie tied Richard's record on October 27, 1963, in the 1,126th game of his career. Ironically, it occurred in the Montreal Forum, and Howe beat goalie Gump Worsley with a shot into the corner of the net.

Then Howe hit a dry spell. It lasted five games, during which he could not buy a goal. But on November 10, in his 1,132nd game, Howe blasted a 30-footer past Charlie Hodge to set a new career record of 545. The record goal was, appropriately, scored at Detroit's Olympia Stadium, and again it was against Montreal.

Gordie Howe went on to compile an unbelievable record in NHL play before he finally announced his retirement from the game on September 8, 1971. His brilliant career had spanned twenty-five years of major-league hockey, and in the vital statistics department he boasted 1,687 regular-season games played, 786 goals scored and 1,023 assists—all records. At one time in his playing career he owned 31 NHL records, and he still has most of them. Gordie won the Hart Trophy as the league's Most Valuable Player six times; he won the Art Ross Trophy as the NHL scoring champion six times; and he had twenty-one consecutive selections on the All Star teams, twelve times on the first team and nine times on the second.

The tough kid from Saskatoon, who almost had his career terminated at the age of twenty-two by a severe brain injury, had fought his way back from the near-fatal blow to become the greatest hockey player of all time. Gordie became the superstar of all superstars for one simple reason—he did not know the meaning of the word "quit."

13

Henry Armstrong . . .
little dynamo of the ring

The date was October 29, 1937. The place was Madison Square Garden in New York City. Henry Armstrong, five feet, seven inches tall and weighing 124 pounds, did a shuffling dance in the corner of the ring, his brown body glistening under the overhead ring lights. This was to be the most important fight yet in his short career, a battle against Petey Sarron, a dark-faced Syrian who was champion of the featherweight division.

Henry Armstrong was aware that he had come a long way to reach this moment, and he had overcome many obstacles to get where he was. He had been born in poverty, had been so small as a young boy that he constantly had to fight off bigger and tougher kids on his block and had chosen the most demanding profession of all in which to make his way—boxing. Now here he was, poised to meet the featherweight champ in a bout for the title—little Henry Armstrong, reaching out to tackle yet another big obstacle. And Petey Sarron was quite an obstacle—a tough, mean young man who would give him the battle of his life. Henry Armstrong knew that this one wasn't going to be any Sunday school picnic.

Henry Armstrong was not his real name. He was born Henry Jackson on December 12, 1912, the youngest of thirteen children in the Jackson family. His father, a sharecropper on a cotton plantation in Mississippi, was a mixture of Indian, Irish and Negro stock. His mother was a full-blooded Iroquois Indian. He was so tiny and scrawny when he was born that his oldest brother looked down at him and said disdainfully, "Gee, Mom, he looks just like a little rat."

His mother was incensed. "He may look like a little rat to you," she said, "but he's going to be a big man some day. Henry is going to be a preacher."

Life was hard for the Jackson family. When the cotton crop was good, the Jacksons lived tolerably well; when the crop was bad, they went hungry. Like all the rest of the family, Henry spent the early part of his life in the effort merely to survive. Henry's father decided to move to St. Louis, Missouri, where it was said that jobs paying good wages could be obtained. Henry was four years old when the family moved. A year later his mother died.

In his early teens, Henry tried to help his father support the family by taking odd jobs around the neighborhood. He knew his mother had wanted him to become a preacher, but studying for the ministry seemed a faraway goal—if it could be achieved at all. Meanwhile, he sold newspapers on a downtown corner, where he had to fight off tough kids who tried to harass him. At sixteen he got a job as a railroad section hand, and it was during this period in his life that the ring began to beckon him. He was pretty handy with his fists, and he thought he might go farther in the ring than he ever could in the pulpit. He fought a few amateur fights in St. Louis and did well despite his small stature.

At seventeen, fighting under the name of "Melody" Jackson,

Henry entered the AAU boxing championships in St. Louis. He survived the preliminaries and finally was matched with a tough Negro kid named Jimmy Birch. On the line was the title of "colored featherweight champ of the west."

The word "colored" was inserted with reason. In those days black and white boys were not permitted to fight each other in St. Louis, so separate championships had to be set up in each weight division for "colored" boys.

Although Henry was to have many memorable fights, his boyhood battle with Jimmy Birch was one he never forgot. One reason was the fact that he was sick before the fight, and felt so weak he was almost afraid to crawl into the ring. But he did, and in the first round Birch went after Henry with everything he had, pumping rights and lefts into his face almost at will.

When the bell rang for the second round, Birch leaped from his stool and plastered Henry with a right to the head. It was the hardest blow of the fight, but Henry did not go down. In fact, he responded to the indignity like a windmill gone berserk. Angry and hurt, he lashed out with both fists, flailing Birch with rights and lefts. Birch failed to survive the attack, and Henry "Melody" Jackson was crowned "colored featherweight champ of the west" by a knockout.

By this time a friend, Harry Armstrong, began handling him. The two of them went to Pittsburgh, where Henry turned professional. For some reason Harry Armstrong didn't want his protégé to go by his own name of Henry Jackson.

"I'll give you my name," he said. "We'll call you Henry Armstrong."

From then on, Henry "Melody" Jackson fought as Henry Armstrong.

Pickings in Pittsburgh, unfortunately, were not very good, and bouts were few.

"We'll go to California," Harry Armstrong decided. "There are plenty of fights to be had out there."

Neither Henry nor his manager had any money, and they hooked rides on freight trains heading west. When they arrived, they began to haunt the gyms. Finally Harry was able to get his fighter some bouts.

In a limited way, Henry Armstrong was a sensation on the Coast. He began to whip featherweights up and down the California coastline, and at one point Al Jolson, the jazz singer and movie star, donated $5,000 to Henry's cause and urged a big-time manager to take over Henry's career. The manager's name was Fat Eddie Mead, a New Yorker with plenty of savvy in the fight business.

Mead immediately took Henry Armstrong to New York and began arranging matches. For almost a year Armstrong put on an exhibit rarely equaled in the fight business. He fought every two weeks, and he defeated one opponent after another. Finally his reputation reached the point where the featherweight champion, Petey Sarron, was forced to meet him for the title.

Now, Armstrong waited impatiently for the first round of the most important fight of his short career. If he could win this one, he would be on his way to a solid career in the ring. And for the first time in his life he would be earning real money. It was his big opportunity, and Henry Armstrong didn't want to muff it.

Referee Arthur Donovan called the two fighters to the center of the ring, made them shake hands and gave them orders to "come out fighting." Armstrong trudged back to his corner

and shed his robe. He would come out fighting, all right. He
planned to do it that way. He would come out swinging with
both fists, hoping to knock Sarron out quickly. He did not intend, or want, to go the full fifteen rounds with the champ
to a decision. In that case, Armstrong felt sure, the champion
would get the nod.

Knocking the champion out was the only sure way to get the
featherweight title.

The bell rang, and both fighters came out quickly. Both
started swinging, like automatons tuned to the same wave-
length, and immediately Armstrong became sure of one thing:
Sarron had the same fight plan! Both were trying to end it
early. That meant a slugfest, and that was right down Armstrong's alley. Because of his nonstop punching, Henry Armstrong had earned himself several nicknames—the Human
Buzz Saw, Hammering Henry, Hurricane Henry, the California Comet and Mr. Perpetual Motion. Now he would have
to live up to those names.

Armstrong fought stoutly, but in the opening rounds the
more experienced Sarron held the edge. Both men threw mur-
derous punches, but more of Sarron's landed. Despite Henry's
efforts, the champ was topping him, winning each round.

For five rounds Henry Armstrong took the worst of the punishment. But toward the end of the fifth round, Henry landed
several hard punches and Sarron's legs buckled a little. It gave
Armstrong ideas. The sixth round would be the deciding one.
The champ was weakening, and Armstrong was certain he
could finish him off in the sixth.

Henry Armstrong was a wild man in the sixth round. He
rushed from his corner and hit Sarron with a hard right. The
champ retreated, and Armstrong pinned him against the ropes.

He rained blow after blow to the face of the befuddled Sarron, finally nailing him with a left uppercut and a right to the chin that deposited the champ on the canvas.

Referee Arthur Donovan moved in quickly for the count.

"One . . . two . . . three . . . four . . ."

Sarron tried to get up, pushing himself erect with his gloved hands. He fell back to his knees.

". . . five . . . six . . . seven . . ."

Sarron was still on his knees, his body weaving.

". . . eight . . . nine . . . ten and out!"

Little Henry Armstrong was the new featherweight champion of the world!

It was a dazzling moment for Henry. He had fought his way up from cheap rooms and unimportant preliminary bouts in Los Angeles to the top of the featherweight division. He could have stopped there and savored his new-found glory, but Henry had other ideas. By putting on a little weight, he could qualify for the lightweight division; then he might move on to the welterweights, and maybe he could go even farther than that! He was a nothing guy who had battled his way to the top of one division. Who could stop him from going on to even greater accomplishments?

Henry Armstrong found, however, that there was a roadblock in his way to the lightweight title. Lou Ambers was the lightweight champion, and he wanted no part of the wild-swinging, vicious little creature known as Hammering Henry. He kept dodging a bout with Armstrong until the frustrated featherweight champ decided to try to make the welterweight limit of 145 pounds.

Barney Ross, a tough and courageous fighter, was the welterweight king. He had fought some of the best—Rocky Kansas, Jimmy McLarnin, Tony Canzoneri—but now he was nearing the end of his career. He wanted one more big-money fight so that he could retire comfortably, and he knew that Henry Armstrong would draw a big crowd. Ross and Armstrong signed a contract for a fight on May 31, 1938, with the welterweight crown at stake.

Ross was a three-to-one favorite to retain his title, but the day belonged exclusively to Henry Armstrong. Although Ross fought like an enraged lion, he was no match for the battering Armstrong. Henry attacked Ross with every punch in his arsenal and never let up. For fifteen grueling rounds the fight went on. At the finish Ross's right eye was swollen and closed, his nose misshapen, his mouth bleeding, his cheekbone bruised. How he managed to hang on for the full fifteen rounds is a boxing miracle; but when it was all over, the courageous Ross had lost his title.

Henry Armstrong was now king of both the featherweight and welterweight divisions!

Still not satisfied, Henry drew a bead on the lightweight title again. Lou Ambers, the champion, was a fine fighter, but he dreaded the thought of meeting the animal called Henry Armstrong. But, in the final analysis, the champion has to defend his title against the leading contender, and the two finally met for the lightweight championship on August 17, 1938, at Madison Square Garden.

Again, Lou Ambers was a three-to-one favorite to beat Armstrong, and the crowd was definitely on the side of the champ. Henry was aware, too, that this might be the toughest fight of his career, for Ambers was an explosive puncher who could cut a man to ribbons.

The fight turned out to be one that boxing will long remember. There was no sparring, no feeling each other out, when the opening bell rang. Both fighters rushed eagerly to ring-center and began to swing away. The crowd howled with excitement as the two fighters slugged it out toe-to-toe.

In the second round Ambers drew first blood. He clouted Henry across the face and opened a cut near his mouth. But Henry would not allow the injury to slow him down. He continued to slug it out with the champ through the third and fourth rounds.

The fifth round was the same—both pounding each other with wild abandon. But just before the bell rang to end the fifth, Henry landed a right cross to Ambers' jutting jaw. Ambers slumped to the canvas, but the bell rang to end the round and save him from a knockout.

In Henry's corner his manager said, "He's about through. You can finish him in the sixth."

Henry took the advice to heart. He rushed out at the bell and rained rights and lefts to Ambers' head. Halfway through the round Henry knocked Ambers down again, but the champ wasn't a quitter. He staggered to his feet at the count of eight and renewed the battle.

In the seventh round Armstrong began throwing punches with such bewildering abandon that two of them were low. The referee took the round away from Henry, and this seemed to encourage Ambers. He came out in the eighth like a new man, cutting Armstrong around the eyes and again opening the cut on his mouth. Henry began to look like a loser, although he was leading the champ on points.

By the tenth round Henry was so bloody that the referee came to his corner and looked him over.

"I'm going to have to stop the fight," he said.

Henry shook his head. "No! I can go on!"

The referee relented, and the fight continued. It went the full route, with both fighters absorbing vicious blows but neither willing to give an inch to the other. When the fight ended, Armstrong was dazed and shaken. Ambers was not as badly marked, but he was near exhaustion. Both knew it would be a close decision.

The two ringside judges turned in their votes. One had Armstrong the winner, eight rounds to six with one even. The other voted for Ambers, eight to seven. The referee's card would determine the winner.

As it turned out, the referee had given seven rounds to Armstrong, six to Ambers, with two even.

The decision had gone to Henry Armstrong. Now he held three titles—featherweight, lightweight and welterweight—the first man in ring history ever to hold three titles at one time! And he had turned the trick in less than a year!

Despite the fact that Henry was now an idol of the ring and could have basked in his glory, he went on fighting at a once-a-month clip. Eventually he relinquished his featherweight crown because he could no longer make the weight, but he went on fighting anyone who would get into the same ring with him. One of these was a roughhouse fighter named Fritzie Zivic, who had his eye on the welterweight championship.

Armstrong and Zivic were signed for a welterweight title match to be held at Madison Square Garden on October 4, 1940, and it turned out to be another memorable battle.

As he did in all his fights, Henry Armstrong rushed out of his corner at the sound of the bell to finish off his opponent in the least possible time. For the first four rounds Armstrong carried the fight, bouncing punches off the retreating Zivic and backing him around the ring. Zivic was obviously trying to stay away from Mr. Perpetual Motion, letting him wear himself out with his own fury. Then, in the fifth, Zivic opened up a little and cut Armstrong over both eyes, and blood gushed down to blind him.

In his corner after the fifth, Armstrong's attendants stopped the bleeding, but in the sixth round Zivic reopened the cuts. The two wounds swelled, and gradually Armstrong's eyes began to close. By the time the eighth round was reached, Henry Armstrong was fighting blindly.

At the end of the eighth, Henry sat in his corner and said, "If I could only see him!" And that was the key to the matter. Armstrong could barely see his tormentor, and from the ninth round through the fourteenth Fritzie Zivic was the one who took charge of the fight.

When the bell rang for the fifteenth and final round, Henry Armstrong, a bleeding, mangled wreck, knew that Zivic was miles ahead of him on points and that he would lose his welterweight title to this tough man unless he could knock him out.

With incredible courage—not to mention recklessness— Armstrong exploded from his corner at the bell and lashed out furiously at his opponent. But Zivic fended him off easily. Just before the bell rang, Zivic unloaded a powerful right to Henry's jaw, and the welterweight champ of the world staggered on wobbly legs and collapsed to the canvas. It was the first time he had been knocked down in his championship career, and even though the bell saved him from an official knockout, he was a beaten man.

Fritzie Zivic was the new welterweight title holder.

In the New York *Herald-Tribune*, sports writer Caswell Adams wrote a tribute to Henry Armstrong that sounded like an epitaph. "Henry Armstrong," he said, "won't be able to fight again for four months, and maybe never will again, but he went out the way the best do—fighting."

Henry Armstrong not only fought again, he was back in

the ring in three months. And who was he fighting? Fritzie Zivic, of course!

In his heart, Armstrong must have known that he was near the end of the line. His reflexes weren't as fast as they had been, his punch had lost some of its zing and he tired in the ring quicker than in the old days. Still, he would not concede that he was finished. He thought he had at least one more good fight left in him, and that he could beat Fritzie Zivic and regain his title.

The largest fight crowd in the history of the Garden came out on the cold night of January 17, 1941, to see the second Armstrong-Zivic battle. It was another bloody spectacle. But from the opening round it became evident that Henry Armstrong was not the bruising fighter he had once been. He had courage, and he tried desperately to put Zivic on the canvas. But Zivic was the master. He danced around Armstrong, jabbing with his left, crossing with his right, making mincemeat of Armstrong for ten heartbreaking rounds. In those ten rounds he opened cuts over both of Henry's eyes again, and knocked him down once in the sixth. And when the tenth round was over, referee Arthur Donovan and a doctor from the State Athletic Commission came to Armstrong's corner.

"Just one more round, Henry," Donovan said. "I can't let it go longer than that."

Henry knew that this was it. He was again faced with the task of knocking Zivic out in the eleventh round or Donovan would stop the fight.

Armstrong raced from his corner and tore into the surprised Zivic. Zivic backed away. In a blind rage, Armstrong smashed lefts and rights to Zivic's head. When the bell rang to end the eleventh round, Zivic was still on his feet—but he staggered uncertainly as he returned to his corner.

Referee Donovan looked at the suddenly revived Henry Armstrong and decided to let the fight continue.

The bell clanged for the twelfth round. Zivic came out of his corner slowly, wary now of this little man who seemed to have so much stamina and power in his body. But he had nothing to worry about. Henry Armstrong had punched himself out in the eleventh round. He had nothing left. Exhausted, he was a setup for the still strong Zivic. Before the round was half over, Zivic knew the truth. He moved in fast for the kill, pounding Henry across the ring, pinning him against the ropes. Armstrong's legs turned to spaghetti, and he staggered drunkenly. Blood ran from his cut eyes, from his nose, from his mouth.

Referee Donovan saw that Armstrong was defenseless and in danger of being seriously hurt, and he stepped in quickly and held the two fighters apart.

The fight was over, and Fritzie Zivic was again the victor.

To all intents and purposes, Henry Armstrong's ring career was over. But since he had carelessly spent all the money he had made in the ring, Armstrong was destitute at the end of the year. There was nowhere he could earn money except in the ring, and Henry tried for a comeback. He fought mostly setups—inferior fighters who were going nowhere—and won 23 of 26 bouts.

The last fighter he met during his comeback attempt was a young boxer named Sugar Ray Robinson. Robinson, who was destined for greatness, beat him badly—and Henry Armstrong retired from the ring a second time.

A year later he tried still another comeback. He won 17 more fights, but when he lost to an unknown fighter of little talent, he retired permanently.

Beaten, discouraged and broke, unable any longer to make

a living with his fists, Henry Armstrong headed for the bottom of the human junkpile. He drank heavily and went down in a fog of alcohol.

One morning in 1950 he woke up in Los Angeles with a terrible headache from drinking and knew he had fallen as low as he could go. Suddenly he remembered that his mother had always wanted him to be a preacher. A preacher, he thought—was that possible? Henry decided to find out. With the same courage he had shown in the ring, he pulled himself erect, gave up alcohol and studied for the ministry.

It was the most important comeback of all. Two years later he was ordained in the Baptist faith. He preached at revival meetings and in churches, and the man who hated everyone in the ring now loved everyone in the world.

At the age of forty-two, the Reverend Henry Armstrong had entered a new profession as "a humble worker of the Lord."

The little man of the ring had shown how big he really was. He had come back from the brink of physical defeat three times during his ring career. But his final comeback—and by far the most important—was a spiritual one. He had conquered the ravages of alcohol to become a preacher of the gospel—just as his mother, so many years before, had predicted.

14

Gertrude Ederle . . .
the girl who didn't have a chance

The pretty nineteen-year-old girl in the red bathing suit stood on the shore at Cape Gris-Nez, France, and gazed out at the choppy waters of the English Channel. It was 6:45 in the morning of August 6, 1926, and within a few minutes the young girl would plunge into the waters of the Channel and attempt to swim the twenty miles to Dover, England.

The prevailing opinion was that she would never make it. Everything was stacked against her. Although many distance swimmers had tried to conquer the turbulent Channel waters, only five had succeeded. The first was Captain Matthew Webb of England, who swam from Dover to Cape Gris-Nez on August 24-25, 1875. Thirty-six years later, on September 5-6, 1911, Thomas W. Burgess of England duplicated Webb's feat. Two successes were registered in August, 1923, when Henry Sullivan of the United States swam from England to France, and Enrico Tiraboschi of Italy swam from France to England, and in September of that same year Charles Toth of the United States made the distance from Cape Gris-Nez to Dover.

But scores of others had tried and failed, and it was believed that only the strongest men with the greatest stamina could hope to make the crossing against the severe obstacles the Channel offered—icy water, choppy waves and strong tides.

Now, here was this slip of a girl—Gertrude Ederle of New York—ready to try what only the strongest men had achieved, and everyone knew it was a foolhardy and hopeless adventure. Numerous women had tried the crossing, but none had succeeded. Gertrude Ederle herself had tried it the previous year and failed. Scores of powerful men swimmers had found it impossible. And shrewd gamblers, who rarely took chances, were posting three-to-one odds that she would never make it.

The fact that the young girl was already a successful competitive swimmer counted for nothing. Gertrude Ederle's biggest obstacle was simply the fact that she was a girl.

Gertrude Caroline Ederle was born in New York City on October 23, 1906, of German parentage. Her father was a butcher, her mother a stalwart housewife. Gertrude learned to swim at the age of eight at Highlands, New Jersey, where the Ederles had a summer home. At ten years of age she won a 50-yard race, and at twelve was considered good enough to become a member of the Women's Swimming Association of New York, the largest organization of its kind in the world.

In 1919, at the age of thirteen, Gertrude won the metropolitan junior 100-yard championship and followed with another victory in a 220-yard race. Then, on August 1, 1922, she established herself as a real queen of the water when she beat 51 rivals in a three-and-one-half-mile event in New York Bay.

From that time on Gertrude (called Trudy by her family) broke a record almost every time she stepped into a pool.

Following the New York Bay victory, she won the national furlong title; in September she bettered seven world records over various lengths, displaying an incredible ability to keep going at top speed no matter how long the race. Then, in 1925, she broke a record that should have erased doubt about her ability to swim in long endurance contests when she swam from the Battery in lower New York to Sandy Hook, New York, in seven hours and eleven minutes, bettering the men's record over the 21-mile distance. She was the first woman ever to conquer the course.

Despite all this, the experts said that the English Channel —a treacherous stretch of water—would prove too much for the 125-pound Gertrude.

At exactly 7:08 A.M., Gertrude Ederle plunged into the foaming waters of the perilous channel to start her swim for glory. Accompanying her was the tug *Alsace*, carrying the American flag and a wireless to transmit messages to the United States during the swim. Aboard the *Alsace* were Gertrude's father; her sister, Margaret (her mother waited in New York for the news); Thomas W. Burgess, who had conquered the Channel in 1911 and was now her trainer; and several other talented swimmers of the day. Behind the tug was another that carried newspapermen, photographers and movie cameramen. As Gertrude cut her way through the water, using the crawl stroke that many swimming experts thought was good only for short speed dashes, she could look up at the *Alsace* and see lettering on the lee side that said, "This Way, Ole Kid!" with an arrow pointing forward.

A sharp wind from the southwest whipped up a rough sea, making Gertrude's start a difficult one. The temperature was 61. Still, with strong, space-eating strokes, she covered the first four miles in three hours. Burgess, worried that her relentless speed might tire her, cautioned her to slow down, to save her strength for what he knew lay ahead. After all, the object was to simply swim the Channel; there was no thought of setting a time record.

Gertrude shook her head at Burgess' suggestion. "I feel good," she responded, and continued to take strong strokes that pushed her through the water with the smoothness and ease of a seal.

A half hour after she had passed the four-mile mark, Gertrude took her first food. It was a light snack consisting of beef extract, which she drank while floating on her back, and some chicken, which she gobbled down hastily.

Those aboard the tug felt it important to keep buoying Gertrude's spirits, and from time to time her sister and two other female swimmers would take to the water to keep her company. Those on the tug sang the "Star Spangled Banner" and scribbled humorous comments on a blackboard they held up for Gertrude to see. When they were not doing this, they shouted words of encouragement.

"We're going to make it," Gertrude, who needed very little encouragement at all, shouted back.

By noon Gertrude's power-packed strokes had carried her to the halfway mark in her effort to swim the Channel. All was going well, and she continued to make progress until 1:30 in the afternoon, when a sudden squall threatened her. Rain, driven by a fierce wind, lashed at her face, and the winds created heavy swells that made it difficult for her to make any progress. Her speed was slowed almost to a stop, but she continued doggedly on. By three o'clock the situation had changed again. The rain was still coming down in a torrent, but the tide was now in her favor. Gertrude found herself almost drifting on the incoming Dover tide. The best estimate at 3 P.M. was that she was nine miles from her goal.

But the English Channel is capricious, casting a favor one minute and impeding the next. The drifting tide lasted only a little while and then, quite suddenly, Gertrude Ederle found herself in trouble. By five o'clock the wind had increased to shrieking fury, blowing against her again. Gertrude fought bravely against the choppy, swirling waters churned up by the wind, her mind tuned to only one thing—stroke, stroke, stroke. But she went nowhere.

Burgess decided this was the right time to give her a short rest with her second meal—this one, hot chocolate.

"How do you feel, Gertie?" he asked apprehensively.

"Fine."

Her quick response brought cheer to her father, and he decided to spur her on. He had promised to buy her a new automobile if she made the swim successfully, and now he leaned over the rail of the tug.

"Trudy," he called, "don't forget you won't get that red roadster unless you get across."

Gertrude flashed him a confident smile from the water.

"Pop," she replied, "I intend to have that roadster."

But by six o'clock the ordeal had grown to such proportions that there was talk of making Gertrude give up the attempt. Burgess was worried about her. The weather was horrible, and the waters had become so rough that the last few miles to the coast seemed impossible to negotiate. In the water, the nineteen-year-old Gertrude was fighting pluckily against rolling waves, gaining a few strokes, then being pushed back several more.

The captain of the tug *Alsace* discussed the situation with Burgess.

"It will be impossible to land the tug at Dover in this weather," he said, "but I might be able to put in at Deal. That would require some four hours more of sailing and plenty of maneuvering."

Burgess walked to the rail and looked down at the struggling girl in the water. He had made up his mind.

"It's impossible," he shouted. "You'll have to come out!"

Gertrude looked up at him in amazement. When she was sure she had heard him right, she shook her head in protest.

"No! No! I intend to go on!" she shouted. And she tried to give renewed impetus to her strokes.

Burgess looked exasperated. "Come out!" he ordered.

Gertrude paid no attention.

She had now been in the water for eleven hours. The sea was frightening, with the winds blowing in savage gusts and the swells impeding all progress. Burgess was convinced that this determined young girl would have to give up, even though eleven hours of effort would go down the drain. He turned to Gertrude's father.

"It's best to take her out and abandon the attempt," he said firmly. But Gertrude's sister, Margaret, objected.

"Trudy hasn't asked to come out yet. She's all right. Let her go on."

But Burgess was adamant. As a man who had negotiated the treacherous waters himself, he knew the peril Gertrude was facing.

"She must come out," he insisted. "I will not take the responsibility of waiting for a sign from her that she wishes to come out."

He turned to the rail again. "Come on out, Trudy!" he shouted.

Again Gertrude shook her head.

"What for?" was her simple question.

Burgess stared in amazement. He had no answer to combat this stubborn girl's grit and determination.

It was 6:30 P.M. now, the beginning of a long three-hour ordeal. In addition to the wind, rain and monstrous swells, a cross tide was hampering her progress. Gertrude's strokes were as powerful as ever, but she could only hold her own. At times she even lost ground. But she would not give up. For more than an hour she fought against the tide, exhibiting stamina such as those on the tug had never before seen. But she was gaining very little distance, and the question in everyone's mind was: How long can she keep it up? How long before she would completely collapse and have to be pulled from the water?

Seven o'clock, eight o'clock—and the plucky girl realized suddenly that the capricious waters of the Channel had changed again. The wind had shifted, and the waters were now heading for the English coast!

Happily, she struck out—stroke after stroke after stroke —determined now to complete her mission. On the *Alsace* the amazed Burgess marveled at the fact that she was still striking out with powerful strokes after enduring hours of battle against the vicious play of water, wind and tide.

"I never saw anyone so marvelous," he said admiringly. "She has done everything."

Having now changed his mind completely, he went to the rail of the tug and cupped his hands to his mouth. "Take your time, Gertie!" he shouted. "It is sure now. You are in this time. I'm certain of it!"

And she was. At exactly 9:40 P.M. she hit shallow water and waded ashore at Kingsdown, England, on the Dover coast. The tug joined her, and on shore there was a tearful reunion. Both her father and sister were crying with joy.

"Trudy! Trudy! You did it!" It was her father, taking her in his arms.

"Trudy! If only Mother were here!" said her sister.

It was a moment to be savored. Gertrude Ederle had not only conquered the unpredictable waters of the English Channel, but had overcome all the obstacles that everyone said were against her. She had beaten the gamblers' three-to-one odds against her; she had beaten the belief that no girl could ever do it; and she had done it in record time.

Gertrude Ederle had crossed the Channel in 14 hours and 31 minutes—the fastest time ever! She had bettered the previous fastest time, set by Italy's Enrico Tiraboschi—16 hours, 33 minutes.

She was not only the first woman to swim the Channel, but the fastest among both men and women!

News of her accomplishment spread across the world, and Gertrude found herself a heroine lauded by every newspaper and magazine published.

All except one.

One London newspaper, convinced that she would never complete her swim across the Channel, pulled one of the great *faux pas* of newspaperdom. On the very day of Gertrude's triumph, the paper put in type a scholarly editorial which stressed the point that it was futile for women to engage in competitive athletics, because they must forever remain athletically inferior to men. When the news that Gertrude Ederle had conquered the Channel reached the newspaper, it was too late to withdraw the editorial.

The newspaper was already on the streets with its hollow story!

That's how sure some people were that Gertrude Ederle would fail.

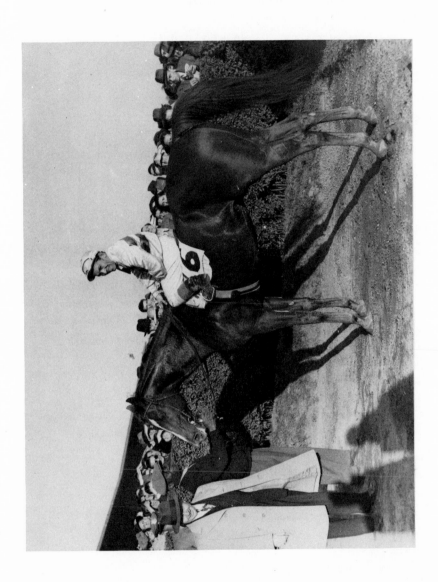

15

Conn McCreary...
the man with a boy's legs

It was Derby Day, 1951, at Louisville, Kentucky. Famous old Churchill Downs, where the race had been run every year since 1875, was spruced up in its best clothes, and the excitement that always hovers over the biggest and most prestigious horse race in the country spread through the crowd like a contagious disease. A large field of twenty sleek horses had paraded around the paddock, and now, to the soft strains of "My Old Kentucky Home," they were moving into position at the starting gates.

Conn McCreary, a midget of a man seated on the sloping back of Count Turf, surveyed the scene with nostalgia. It was a replay, he thought, of something that had occurred a long time ago—so long ago that it seemed like a dream. He had won the Kentucky Derby seven years before, in 1944, on a horse named Pensive. He had taken Pensive into the Preakness and had won that too. At Belmont, however, he finished second, and the elusive Triple Crown of racing slipped from his grasp. Still, the three races had catapulted him to fame almost overnight, and Conn McCreary became the biggest name in horse racing.

Four years later he was nobody.

Conn McCreary's slide into obscurity began in a subtle way at first. With an impressive list of wins behind him, he suddenly started to lose. Instead of coming home a winner, he began missing by a hair. This happened so repeatedly, the word quickly went around that Conn McCreary had lost his touch. Where previously horse owners clamored for his services, he was now no longer in demand. No one wanted him to ride for them any longer. Trainers who had once greeted him with smiles turned away in embarrassment, not knowing what to say to a man who had hit the top and then fallen so low. Finally, McCreary had dropped out of racing entirely, and for a year he was idle, a down-and-outer who hung around the tracks because racing had been his world and he knew of nowhere else to go.

But just when things looked gloomiest, an angel had come along—an angel in the form of a man named Jack Amiel, who wanted him to ride Count Turf in the 1951 Derby. McCreary could hardly believe it, but he seized the opportunity, and now the big moment had come. He was back in the Derby with a chance to prove to those who thought he was washed up that he could still handle a horse.

Gently, Conn McCreary coaxed Count Turf into the starting gate and sat nervously, waiting for the gates to open and spew forth the twenty horses that would make this year's Derby look like a cavalry charge. He was going to do his best to win, he knew that. But he was of a practical nature, and he was aware that his best might not be enough.

Count Turf was a 15-1 underdog.

There were two occasions in the life of Conn McCreary when he could have thrown up his hands in despair and quit. One was when he was very young and already realized that he would never grow to the size of an average man. The other was when his career fell apart and there was nothing to look forward to but days of frustration and poverty. But McCreary was made of tough stock, and the word "quit" was not in his vocabulary.

Born in St. Louis, Missouri, Conn McCreary was raised in a rough neighborhood known as Kerry Patch. When he was about ten years old, it dawned on him that he would never grow up. The top part of his body had developed normally, but his legs were weak and misshapen. In his teens he weighed only 90 pounds, and his height was only four-feet-eight. He was muscular from the waist up, but his spindly legs were stunted and his measurement from waist to ground was just over thirty inches.

He was a young man with the legs of a boy.

Knowing he would never grow any taller, Conn McCreary decided to enter a profession where being small was an asset. He liked horses and decided to become a jockey. The only trouble was that he knew nothing about horses or riding. Still, he had a determination much bigger than his size, and when he was fifteen years old he quit school and headed for Lexington, where the great horse farms of Kentucky were located.

Fate led him to the Woodvale Farm, where he asked Steve Judge, a trainer, for a job. Judge looked the little fellow over.

"Ever work around horses before?" he asked.

"No," Conn said. "But I can learn. I want to be a jockey."

Steve Judge liked the boy's determination and took him on. Conn served his apprenticeship in the world of horses well. He went to work hauling water, cleaning out the stalls and exercising the horses. It was tough work, but Conn never complained. It was obvious to Judge that he had a way with horses, a feeling for them that came naturally, and after a while he allowed Conn to ride the horses in morning workouts.

It was during these morning jaunts that McCreary found that his tiny legs were a handicap to him. Most jockeys have normally proportioned bodies, except that they are smaller and weigh less than the average man. Conn was man-sized only in the upper part of his body, and he discovered that when he was riding a horse his tiny legs were of no help in gripping the horse's sides. Until he learned to adapt to this situation, he was in constant danger of slipping from the horse's back. He had to use the strength in his arms and shoulders as a substitute for his legs, but he quickly mastered this unorthodox riding technique and convinced the trainers at Woodvale that he could handle a horse in his own special manner. He convinced them so well, in fact, that in 1939, when he was eighteen years old, they permitted him to ride in competition.

The race took place at Arlington in Chicago. Young McCreary was up on a horse named Florence M.—a filly that had never won a race.

But then, neither have I, Conn thought, and the young rider brought the horse down the stretch in the lead and held on to win the race.

Despite this initial victory, most trainers and jockeys doubted that the tiny McCreary (smaller even than other riders) would ever make a good jockey. Only Steve Judge had confidence in him, and he began to give young McCreary better horses to ride, watching him closely and noticing improvement in every race.

In the fall of 1941, when Conn was twenty, Judge gave him a two-year-old champion named Our Boots, the horse that started McCreary on the road to fame. Conn rode him in the Blue Grass Stakes at Keeneland and won.

That was the beginning. That same winter he went to Florida, rode horse after horse during the winter racing season and did so well that his name became famous within a few months. The big stables began to demand his services, and before long he was riding on some of the country's most famous tracks.

He was a favorite of horse owners, and he was the jockey that fans went to see. His popularity stemmed not only from the fact that he was so tiny (people instinctively like to see the little guy beat the big one), but also from the technique he used in winning his races. His race plan was to hang back at the beginning, saving his horse while the rest of the field ran wildly ahead of him. He had nerves of steel, and disciplined himself and his mount to stay behind until the last possible moment. When it came, he made his move, rushing up through the pack, overtaking the leaders and beating them all to the finish line.

Race after race was won in this come-from-behind fashion, and finally he became known as "the kid with the clock in his head." The expression meant simply that he knew just when to make his move so that he would overtake the leaders and get under the wire on top.

It was a dangerous way to race. If he waited too long before making his move, the opportunity to overtake the front-runners would be gone. On the other hand, if he moved too soon, his horse might run out of steam before he could reach the finish line. McCreary knew the precise moment to move—the "clock in his head" told him.

So it was that Conn McCreary had the world of horse racing at his feet, and in 1944 he took a few steps to cement his position as one of the top jockeys in the land. That year he donned the red-and-blue silks of the famous Calumet Farm, riding

Pensive to a win in the Kentucky Derby and the Preakness. Seeking the Triple Crown, Conn rode his usual race at Belmont, lagging behind and then coming down the home stretch at top speed to overtake the weary horses ahead of him—but this time he didn't quite make it. A horse named Bounding Home bounded home ahead of him.

Nevertheless, the Derby and Preakness wins and the near-miss at Belmont made him one of the country's top jockeys. Fame and money came to him in abundance. Horse owners and trainers groveled at his feet. The fans asked for autographs, wanted to shake his hand, desired to be seen with him.

The good fortune lasted four years and then, little by little, the fans and the owners and the trainers who had idolized him began to forget about him. Just when it all started nobody can say for certain, but after four years of riding the crest he began to lose more races than he won. The horse owners who had been avid for his services suddenly shunned him, the people who idolized him were strangely gone and the fame and the money both began to diminish.

McCreary could not understand why he was losing. He was running the same racing pattern he had perfected, taking it easy and then coming on fast at the finish. But now it wasn't working. He was starting his rush a little late and was unable to overtake the leaders—and he was finishing out of the money instead of in it.

That famous "clock in his head" was failing him, his superb timing was off, his touch was gone.

Once, after a particularly galling loss, a writer covering the race made a famous remark. He said: "If they put Conn Mc-Creary up on the horse that night instead of Paul Revere, we'd still be subjects of the King of England." Another racing man said: "I don't even consider him a jockey any more. He's just so much dead weight on a horse's back. I don't know what's happened to him."

Conn McCreary's precipitous tumble from one of the best jockeys in the country to one of the worst was a psychological disaster. As he continued to lose, he lost faith in himself. Trying to correct what was wrong without knowing exactly what it was threw him into utter confusion. He began to make mistakes, and it looked as if he would have to learn to ride a horse all over again.

One season in Saratoga he experienced a discouraging number of mishaps—three falls from his horse in two weeks. The second occasion was extremely embarrassing. The horses were in the starting gates and George Cassidy, the starter, was about to press the button to open the gates when McCreary called frantically, "I'm not ready yet, Mr. Cassidy! Not ready!"

But his plea came too late. Cassidy's finger hit the button and the gates flew open. The horses rushed forward, including McCreary's. But Conn wasn't in the saddle. One foot had been out of a stirrup as the horse bounded forward, and McCreary was thrown against the side of the stall and fell to the ground. The riderless horse set out after his competitors.

The next accident, a couple of days later, was even more mortifying. This time the starting gates were right in front of the grandstand, so that thousands of people saw the farce. As the field broke free of the gates, Conn McCreary slipped sideways on his mount and fell to the ground. His horse headed down the track without a rider. McCreary was not hurt and he picked himself up without trouble, but his anger was a seething thing. An attendant picked up Conn's hat and whip and handed them to him. He threw the cap to the ground and stomped on it in a frenzy; then beat himself across his crooked legs with the whip, apparently blaming them for his fall. The

crowd thought it was a humorous, rather than pitiful, sight—
and laughed. Conn was humiliated and rushed off the track
red-faced.

At this point Conn McCreary had reached his lowest ebb.
There seemed no use in continuing. Luck was against him,
and he was fearful that he might never ride another winner—
certainly not in a big race like the Derby. But by this time he
had collected a wife and four children, and it was these loved
ones who kept him racing. After all, a man had to feed his
family, and racing was the only way he knew how to do it.

As an example of how badly things were going, one day
Conn drew four mounts that were better-than-average horses.
He thought perhaps he could win with them and turn his luck
around. But it was the worst day of his career. He won with
the first horse, but was disqualified on a technicality. He rode
the second horse to victory, too, but a few minutes after he
crossed the finish line he was informed that he had been suspended from racing for ten days for an infraction of the rules
in the first race. He was permitted to finish out the day, however, and the third race almost finished him. He was thrown
again coming out of the gate and fractured his skull. Another
jockey took his mount in the stakes race and won it.

"It was a great day for me," he said later. "I got a disquali-
fication, a suspension, a fractured skull and missed out on
10 per cent of a big purse in the stakes race!"

Because there was nothing else he could do, Conn McCreary
continued to race—on small, unimportant tracks. The intervals
between races grew longer and longer; it seemed nobody
wanted to take a chance on him. By the spring of 1950 he was
down and out, a hanger-on at the tracks. Like a magnet, the
Kentucky Derby drew him to Louisville. If he could only get
a horse, if somebody would agree to use him—well, maybe he

could straighten everything out with one brilliant victory in the Big One. But no one wanted him. He found himself a dingy room in a second-rate hotel and stayed there for several days. He remembered how, in 1944, he had been to all the Derby parties and had been the big man at them. Now he was invited to none of them.

Conn McCreary virtually dropped out of sight, then, for a year. In the spring of 1951, unemployed and with his finances impaired, he tried to get a job exercising horses, as he had done as a boy at the Woodvale Farm. He was no longer seeking a horse to ride in a race; he was now satisfied just to be around horses. He was glad to clean the barns, walk the horses and do the unpleasant chores associated with a horse farm. He took a job exercising and training horses for a man named Sol Rutchick who handled horses for a number of owners.

One of the horses he trained was Count Turf.

Count Turf was owned by Jack Amiel, a New Yorker who knew little about horses but wanted badly to enter the 1951 Kentucky Derby. Amiel had great confidence in his horse, but he needed an experienced jockey. His eyes fell on Conn Mc-Creary. With McCreary—a down-and-out jockey eager to make a comeback—riding Count Turf, Amiel felt, there was a good chance of bringing the horse home a winner.

One day he approached Conn and asked him to ride Count Turf in the Derby. The request astounded McCreary, and at first he shook his head in dismay.

"You don't want me," he said. "I'm poison. Don't you know that?"

Amiel just smiled. "I've heard it but I don't believe it," he replied. "With me, you're a good jock. Without you, Count Turf can't win. With you, he can."

It was quite a statement to make, because Count Turf was

a so-so horse that had won only four times in his last twenty starts and had never raised the eyebrows of horse experts anywhere. Only a man who was out of his mind would predict that Count Turf could win the Derby.

Nobody else gave him a chance.

A crowd of 85,000 fans showed up at the venerable Churchill Downs for the 77th running of the Kentucky Derby. Conn McCreary sat aboard Count Turf in the starting gates and thought briefly about the fickleness of fame. He had been on top once before and then had hit rock bottom. Now he was up there again, taking part in the biggest of races. It was an inspiring moment for Conn McCreary, a moment he had never expected to experience again. Still, he had no illusions about his chances of winning. He was realistic enough to know that Count Turf was not a great horse. But he intended to coax every last ounce of effort out of his mount—and maybe, just maybe, they might finish in the money.

The only thing he was sure of was that he'd give Count Turf —a 15-to-1 underdog—the ride of his life.

Suddenly the gates opened, and the twenty horses in the race charged forward. Count Turf hesitated slightly before leaving the gate, and he was next to last when he got started. A grim thought crossed Conn McCreary's mind. *I'll have to come from behind, the way I used to. Will I be able to? Or will the "clock" fail me again?*

In the first half mile of the mile-and-a-quarter race, Count Turf picked up some ground. But he was still back in the pack, in eleventh place.

Moving around the curve and heading up the back stretch, McCreary knew what he had to do. He would have to move up through the field, not with an all-out charge but with a calculating coolness, so that when he came into the home stretch he could make his final drive to overtake the two or three horses still ahead of him. To his delight, Count Turf responded quickly to a soft application of the whip. On the back stretch he passed horse after horse, moving up steadily. In the press box a reporter said, "That's McCreary on Count Turf. That's the way he used to ride. Always coming up fast after hanging behind. You think he can do it?"

"I doubt it," another writer said, peering through binoculars. "He hasn't done it very often in the last seven years. And he's had some good mounts too. McCreary's washed up—and I can't understand why Amiel is using him."

But McCreary was far from finished. By the time he entered the home stretch, there were only two horses—Phil D. and Repertoire—leading him.

It was then that Count Turf tried to pull up, as if he had run enough and wanted to call the whole thing off. But McCreary was not having any of that. He busted the horse across the flanks with the whip a couple of times, and Count Turf sprang forward as if he had been struck from behind by lightning. He slipped by the two leading horses with surprising ease and headed for the final wire.

And he hit the finish line with room to spare!

Count Turf, under a masterful ride by Conn McCreary, had run the mile-and-a-quarter in 2:02.35, the fourth fastest time in the history of the Kentucky Derby!

Both Count Turf and McCreary were draped with roses in the winner's circle as flashbulbs exploded around them. Any jockey who wins the Derby knows the thrill of that moment, but to Conn it was something extra special.

Conn McCreary had surmounted two giant obstacles on his way to success—his cripped legs and his decline into obscurity —and he was back on top.

Courage had been the factor that put him there.

Epilogue

There are other athletes, not mentioned in the preceding pages, who overcame difficulties to star again in their particular sport.

I recall that Billy Martin, the talented infielder of the New York Yankees, was once considered too little to play major-league ball. Ernie Nevers, All American fullback for Stanford University, suffered two broken legs in one season but played in the Rose Bowl that year. Elgin Baylor played pro basketball with two bad knees. Jackie Pung, the Hawaiian woman golfer, suffered a nervous breakdown but came back to continue her professional career. And Mario Andretti, one of the finest automobile racers of our time, was so small that they had to build up the seat in his car so he could see where he was going. These are some I remember; there may be others I'm not aware of.

At any rate, the fifteen stories I chose seem to me to be the most dramatic examples in sport of fortitude under adverse conditions. They are inspiring examples to all of us.

About the Author

Hal Butler was born in St. Louis, Missouri, but moved to Detroit, Michigan, as a child and has spent most of his life there. Educated in the public schools, he got his first writing experience as a reporter for his high school newspaper.

Always too much of a lightweight to actively participate in major sports, he nevertheless played most sports as a youngster and has kept close to the sports scene during his adult life. His writing career has been one of great variety for the past twenty years, including sport and detective fiction as well as non-fiction on sports, travel, history, adventure, automobiles and general subjects. Mr. Butler's stories have appeared in *Saturday Evening Post, Coronet, Pageant, Sport, True, American Mercury* and several foreign publications.

At the present time he serves as managing editor on the *Ford Times*, a national travel magazine published by the Ford Motor Company. He and his family live in Southfield, a suburb of Detroit, and commute during the summer months to a log cabin in northwestern Michigan. Other than writing, Mr. Butler's favorite avocation is travel, having visited most of the continental United States, Hawaii, Europe, Mexico, Canada and the Caribbean.